Campus of the Future
Conference on Information Resources

Wingspread Conference Center
June 22–24, 1986

Co-sponsored by
OCLC Online Computer Library Center
Dublin, Ohio
The Johnson Foundation
Racine, Wisconsin

Online Computer Library Center
6565 Frantz Road
Dublin, Ohio 43017–0702

ISBN: 1-55653-010-2

Printed in the United States of America

1 2 3 4 5 6 7   90 89 88 87

Campus of the Future
Conference on
Information Resources

OCLC Library, Information, and Computer Science Series

Contents

Appendixes, 133

Dear Colleagues:

It is my pleasure to introduce this summary publication from the June 1986 conference entitled "Information Resources for the Campus of the Future." OCLC is many things to many people, but our roots are in the academic community and a significant part of our future lies there as well.

For some time OCLC has been studying the impact of the converging information technologies, including computers, telecommunications, graphics, and their attendant software, on academic institutions in both teaching and research. We have been in the forefront of the transformation of the library that has resulted from these technologies. But, we believe there is an equally transforming impact upon the educational institution as a whole, in which the library has historically played an important role; and, in our judgment, one which it will continue to play.

We have been urging for some time that academic institutions give greater attention to integrated planning of their information needs involving the administration, faculty, library, computing, and communication resources, and addressing the manifold economic issues that arise in this new environment. The Higher Education Policy Advisory Committee to OCLC enthusiastically endorsed the concept of a conference that would bring together these parties in a retreat environment to explore and to share how this is taking place in some pioneering efforts by some of the research universities in the United States, Canada, and the United Kingdom. With the help of the Committee's planning, participation of many of its members, and the generous support of The Johnson Foundation, which made available the splendid facilities and resources of Wingspread, this precedent-setting conference took place on June 22-24, 1986.

What we heard and learned at Wingspread either confirmed our own agendas or raised new issues for us to explore and consider. OCLC may have a number of roles to play in the future information environment. We are doing much thinking and planning, using an iterative process that is the hallmark of OCLC's planning process. We welcome your comments in regard to our role as a facilitator for libraries and for making available scholarly information.

As you read the presentations and summaries in this volume, you will undoubtedly be challenged to think of the future of your own institution. Plans are being made to stage a series of workshops or conferences across the country that will be patterned after the team approach used at the Wingspread Conference and will have a similar focus. Perhaps your institution will be a participant in one of these.

My thanks go to members of the Higher Education Policy Advisory Committee to OCLC and to all of those involved in the conference. The approach was an experiment and one that worked well.

Sincerely,

Rowland C. W. Brown
President

Preface

This publication is a brief summary of a series of significant events
that began in 1984 with the creation of the Higher Education Policy
Advisory Committee to OCLC. It was at the urging of the members
of this Committee that OCLC planned for the conference entitled "Information Resources for the Campus of the Future" that was held at
Wingspread, the Conference Center of The Johnson Foundation, on June
22-24, 1986.

The conference was unique in one major aspect: the participants
were members of university teams that included the president, the chief
academic officer, the director of the library, the director of the computing
center, and a faculty member. It was a condition suggested by the Higher
Education Policy Advisory Committee that only those institutions willing to come as teams be invited to participate in the conference. A few
additional persons were also invited to attend because of special skills
or expertise they would bring to the conference.

Prior to the conference, OCLC staff were able to meet with representatives of most of the participating teams to discuss the agenda and the
format of the meeting. In this way, the conference was shaped to reflect
the character and interests of the participants. The format of the meeting
included open discussions focused on general concerns related to providing information resources for the campus of the future. These general
meetings resulted in discussion questions that served as focal points for
small group meetings of two or three teams.

It was in the small group meetings that much of the substantive
discussion took place. So as to avoid any condition that might inhibit
frank discussion, the small group sessions were not recorded, nor were
detailed reports made. The format and the conditions worked and, in
some instances, provided opportunities for the teams to consider mutual-
ly the information resource problems and issues they face and some of
the approaches that might be used to meet the problems.

This book provides a glimpse of the conference by presenting the
formal portions of the meeting. Talks by Drs. Cyert of Carnegie-Mellon

and Glicksman of Brown, transcriptions of which are included in this book, were given at the opening session as thought-provoking position statements. Both institutions are in close agreement on the importance of providing computerization and easily accessible information resources to members of the campus community, but these presentations brought out the fact that, despite their basic agreement, there are differing philosophies of and approaches to the implementation of their objectives.

The paper by Evelyn Daniel focuses on the ever present concern about supplying information to the campus community and the changes that have occurred and are occurring on the campus as a result of the need or desire for information by a widely diverse constituency. Douglas Van Houweling's paper is a survey of the changes that have occurred in the technical environment, again focused on the impact on providing information resources. Neither of these papers was presented in full at the conference but rather was given to the participants in advance of the meeting and abstracted by the author at the meeting itself.

The conference participants deserve much of the credit for its success. However, much of the preliminary work of the conference was done by Beckie Purdy of OCLC in conjunction with Kay Mauer of The Johnson Foundation. Mary Taylor, Rick Limes, and Lois Yoakam of OCLC were also heavily involved in the preliminary work. We are grateful for their efforts and for the efforts of the many others who provided so much assistance.

Michael J. McGill
Vice President
Research and Technical Planning

Campus
of the
Future

Summary of
Proceedings

T he Higher Education Policy Advisory Committee to OCLC held an invitational conference on Information Resources for the Campus of the Future on June 22–24, 1986. The conference, co-sponsored by The Johnson Foundation, was held at the Wingspread Conference Center in Racine, Wisconsin. The purpose of the conference was to consider the next generation of university information systems and the resources that will be required to provide them.

Rowland Brown, OCLC, (left) and Henry Halstead, The Johnson Foundation

June 22, evening

The conference began with a welcome by sponsors Henry Halstead, The Johnson Foundation, and Rowland C. W. Brown, OCLC. The opening presentations on Educational Imperatives and Information Services for Campuses featured Richard Cyert, President of Carnegie-Mellon University, and Maurice Glicksman, Provost of Brown University. These presentations were intended to stimulate debate and/or exploration of diverse institutional approaches in applying technology to the educational and research functions of the university of the future.

In his opening remarks Richard Cyert stated that there is a revolution under way in American education. He defined a *revolution* as a new
way of achieving bold objectives. He noted that the goal of a university
is to graduate educated men and women. To meet this goal, we must
use new tools that are now being developed. Two parts comprise the
revolution: the first part is to construct new types of computer systems,
including the development of workstations; the second part is to make
the system meet the educational goal.

Cyert noted that the new type of computer system goes beyond the
time-sharing environment of most current university systems, which, he
said, have never been right for universities and, in fact, have the seeds
of their own destruction. The intent is to educate more users, but more
users on a computer system implies more contention for computing
resources, which in turn, implies less responsiveness to its users. This flaw
is overcome by imposing a series of restrictions on users that limit their
access to the computer system. The use of workstations with significant
processing and storage alleviates these restrictions. However, the university still needs "a computer system." A user's workstation needs to be
connected to other workstations and to the university computer system
to allow the user access to large databases. A network of workstations
is now within our reach, and such a system can complete file transfers
and provide access to all members of the campus community.

According to Cyert, one requirement for the success of computer
systems is the development of appropriate standards. These standards
must ensure that the computer system is as useful as today's textbook.
A wide range of intellectual processing is needed to develop solutions
to problems and this processing can transfer understanding between
disciplines. It is not just knowledge that is needed but how to use that
knowledge.

Cyert further stated that computers can have an impact on the
educational environment by facilitating deeper comprehension by
students. The computer allows more complexity and better mechanisms
of visualization through graphics. Computers can provide an enhanced
ability to use knowledge, better teaching through the use of intelligent
tutors, and greater opportunities for students to learn on their own.

In conclusion Cyert noted that the computer revolution affects all
fields, including the humanities, sciences, and social sciences. Computer
databases and simulations can pose questions and allow students to find
the answers.

Following Dr. Cyert, Maurice Glicksman then stated that technology
should serve society and not the reverse. However, it not clear that the
simple introduction of computers into the classroom will accomplish this.
He noted that there is, in fact, little research on the educational process
per se. The goals of higher education from his perspective are: (1) the
creation of knowledge, (2) the communication of knowledge, and (3)
conservation of knowledge. Scientific research enhances the goals of

higher education by improving the quality of knowledge, by providing a quick feedback mechanism, and by delving into complex problems. However, educators are fundamentally conservative, thus the use of newer technology and of data must be quantitatively and qualitatively justified. Glicksman asserted that the current data about the use of technology in the educational environment cannot by itself justify the use of that technology. It is not known, he said, what the conservation of knowledge costs or how much technology saves. However, it is known that personal and professional communication is enhanced by using technology. According to Glicksman, whether technology improves the teaching process is an unanswered question. More must be known about the instructional process to begin with.

June 23, morning

The morning session began with a presentation by Evelyn Daniel based on her paper "An Examination of Faculty and Administrative Knowledge Workers and Their Major Information Support Units." Daniel, Dean of the School of Library Science, The University of North Carolina at Chapel Hill, has studied the users of information systems through research projects.

In describing the changing academic scene, Daniel reported that the university is becoming a more businesslike operation, but faculty members are frequently not involved in strategic planning. There are issues of control and hard trade-offs that must be made. Colleges and universities are increasingly open to influences from the business world. In contemplating such environmental changes, Daniel asked, if a university were to be formed now, how would it be different?

Daniel stated that the campuses of the future will be different. The role of new technology is certainly costly, but delay in the use of technology is also costly. There is a higher proportion of poorly prepared students in today's universities than there was, for example, in the 1950s. Professional schools have increased their populations significantly and today the university sees different proportions of faculty, students, and resource allocations than were true in the past. Part-time faculty in some institutions, for example, comprise about one-third of the total faculty. Minority faculty member numbers are diminishing.

Daniel drew a number of similarities between the computing center and the library. Both the computing center and the library, for example, are concerned about their relationship with their users; both are providing a wide range of new services; both are incurring significantly increased costs; and both are experiencing rising interdependencies which lead to a lack of perceived direction and a lack of unity among their staffs. It is reasonable to conclude that the computer revolution has barely begun. The social and organizational consequences for the university will be far reaching.

Following Daniel's presentation, Anne Firor Scott, Duke University, led a discussion of relevant issues. The following key points were made:

- It is uncertain what impact the new technology and the existence of the computer networks will have on establishing or maintaining cohesiveness in campus communities. A lack of sharing may lead to social and intellectual fragmentation. It is important to consider carefully what is to be gained by driving the university toward a single system of development for the library, research, and administration.

- The process of integrating campus computing enhances the interaction between faculty and across disciplines. While faculty wish to remain a separate and unique element of the campus community, they genuinely welcome this interaction, and they do not want horizontal organizations. Faculty members simply want to be valued, and just bringing people together helps.

- In the library, technology has caused cohesiveness by forcing the sharing of concerns among various elements of the campus community as new technology is evaluated.

- In the changing technological and academic scene, the university is open to a much wider community. The library, for example, is being used by technical firms which are geographically close to the university. Networks may in fact alter the university community. Considering the roles of various elements of the campus community in providing information services, there is concern that faculty may themselves become "service organizations" when they provide general access to their private or semiprivate databases.

- There may be a gap between universities that have access to new technology as compared with those who do not have access. Using technology may cause the generation of a "have" and "have not" society even within the university.

Following this session, small groups continued the discussion of these issues focusing on the needs of their user communities. Appendix C lists questions which were given to conference participants to stimulate discussion.

June 23, afternoon

The afternoon session began with a brief presentation by Douglas Van Houweling, University of Michigan. He stated that the attendance of so many campus decision makers suggests an interest in and a need for strategic focus on a single national higher education information network rather than several networks that have difficulty interconnecting. The need is obviously well understood as is the necessity of a shared strategy. The strategies will probably be incorrect, but will help make day-to-day decisions.

Van Houweling pointed out that the technology being discussed is neutral but its application is not. The technology provides an improved opportunity for intellectual exchange and we are beginning to use the technology for communication. There is an opportunity in scholarship for a "new library" that is connected to all of the other components of the campus and contains algorithmic information, art, and other visual information. There is an opportunity more readily to distribute the results of campus research and knowledge development, he said. He sees these opportunities as based on the traditional strengths of libraries and their ability to preserve, classify, and provide access to all kinds of information. In fact, there is an opportunity for national sharing of information and knowledge, but this will require a set of standards for information networks. Van Houweling asked whether it will be possible for these universities to collaborate to achieve these goals, whether universities will be able to do more than just collectively cope.

During the discussion session that followed, these key points were made:

- Much information comes to faculty that never gets to the library. If libraries never receive this information, it will probably never be made available nationally or internationally.

- Libraries need to focus on current knowledge as well as past history. Libraries must be willing to collect and provide access to work-in-progress. This presents an inherent conflict with the archival function of the library. There are issues of scholarly control (Do scholars want to share their papers?) and logistics (How do we avoid clogging the system? Can we weed?). The economic and psychological ramifications of transition must be recognized.

- The handling of the new information environment is not purely a library problem, it is an institutional problem. It calls not for trading library functions but for trading institutional priorities. The library's old role of acquirer of information must be balanced with the new role of finder/provider of information. The successful library of the future will emphasize information service, not collection development. The library of the future is here *today* in terms of problems that exist. Choices are expensive. This is reality and must be dealt with.

- Where current information is not available in libraries, information networks spring up. If the library does not become more vital and current, the library's role will diminish.

June 24, morning

The wrap-up session was moderated by Joe Wyatt, Vanderbilt University. Each institution had an opportunity to identify what it regarded as the important issues that arose from this conference.

- There is rapid growth in the electronic access to information, and interactions among various elements of the campus community should continue. Legal and policy issues arising from changes in information technology are causing tensions between libraries, authors, and publishers. For example, where do we go from here with educational software that presents special kinds of publishing problems? There is a clear need for standardization so software can be moved/shared from place to place. Book publishers are not likely to take risks, and other professions, including librarianship, are in a state of transition. Librarians must deal with the old and the new, with books and electronic networks.

• In the interaction between a university's library and computing center, each institution should be allowed to do what it does best but have the flexibility to determine who can do that best. The university faces a tremendous demand for computing resources and should look outward toward collaboration.

• Rather than a movement toward applying new technology to the traditional educational and research functions of universities, there is really a revolution under way. Institutions should pay attention to how technology helps them achieve the goals of higher education. The standardization of software that is needed is similar to that of textbooks. Standard languages and operating systems will prevent people in different places from reinventing the wheel. It would be beneficial to hold a future conference which includes demonstrations of existing educational software and sharing of ideas and techniques which take advantage of the new educational tools being developed.

• The development and control of information resources has become a key policy area on university campuses, and "people problems" such as training need attention. In addition, educational software is expensive and the costs must be justified. There

must be more focus from the beginning of the development of new information systems. This is a difficult issue with little precedent. One reason so many university presidents took time to participate in this conference is that the development of information resources is one of the key issues of this decade.

- Faculty will play a key role in pushing the university toward development of new information systems. It may be a good time to push computer instruction. Past work has been hampered by the lack of computing storage capacity, the lack of high-resolution output devices, and the minimal processing power that was available. Electronic publishing is likely to spread like wildfire.

- The library of the future is *now,* and libraries must retool to make the transition to the new information environment. Libraries have typically been the resources for their users, and computing centers have been resources for numerical databases, but this is changing and the two are drawing more closely together.

- The conference was useful because it brought the right people together. Information commitments among organizations are typically very good and they are honored. Although the conference participants spent little time on the economic issues involved, the idea of developing a cooperative venture for instructional software was applauded.

- Information is expensive and will remain so, and it is important how universities shift resources to adapt to new information systems. Central funding assists in planning, but the technology is changing so fast that if institutions react to the changes organizationally, the technology will have changed by the time decisions are made.

Rowland C. W. Brown, OCLC, concluded the conference by noting the dynamics of the group's interaction. By building on the strength of such collaborative efforts, OCLC finds direction to meet the changing needs of higher education.

Papers and Presentations

Why I Believe There Is a Revolution Under Way in Higher Education

Richard M. Cyert
Carnegie-Mellon University

Dr. Cyert was appointed President of Carnegie-Mellon University after ten years as Dean of the Graduate School of Industrial Administration (GSIA). He joined Carnegie-Mellon as an instructor of economics after earning a doctorate from Columbia University. His bachelor's degree is from the University of Minnesota. He was an officer in the U.S. Navy and an instructor at the University of Minnesota and the City University of New York. He has authored or co-authored eight books and has written approximately 100 articles for professional journals in the fields of economics, behavioral science, and management. He has gained international recognition for his studies in economics and management science and has been a consultant in these fields in Belgium, Germany, and Australia.

G iven the title of my talk, some of you might feel like the American who was one of three persons, a Frenchman, a Japanese man, and an American, being executed. The executioner went around to give everyone a last request. The Frenchman said he wanted to hear the "Marseillaise" one more time; the Japanese man said he wanted to hear a lecture on Japanese management once more before he died. The American said, "My request is that I be executed before the Japanese. I can't stand another lecture on Japanese management!" I apologize to those of you who have this feeling about what I'm going to say, but I feel strongly about it and want to make sure that my position is made known. I hope it will be close to that of everybody else.

What I would like to do is to show why I think there is a revolution under way. My definition of a revolution is: the development of a new way of achieving bold objectives. I would emphasize that our objective in universities is to graduate educated men and women. Our aim is to educate the men and women in our organizations. To do that, we now have new tools and new ways of achieving our objectives. This is a revolution. It is not a time for cautious optimism or for any kind of caution; it is a time for recognizing what we want to do and for bold action.

I see this revolution as consisting of two parts, and it is important that both parts be recognized. The first part is the construction of a new kind of computer system for our universities based on the personal computer. The second part is using the personal workstation in education. Let's look first at the computer system.

New Computer System

Most of us have a time-sharing system on our campuses, probably supplemented now with many personal workstations, but it is the time-sharing system that we would probably refer to as our computer system. Time-sharing has never been the right system for universities. I've often said that I would be willing to wager a great deal of money that if anyone were to take a survey at any given time across all universities in the country, 95–99 percent of the faculty respondents would say that they have a terrible computer system on their campuses. The presidents of universities responding would say, "I never spent so much money on anything as I have on computing." This is the way these people react. The reason is clear: a time-sharing system is a system that carries within it the seeds of its own destruction. It is not the right system for a university because our objective is to educate, and that means developing new users and spending time to educate more people to use the computer. But, as soon as we get more users, we increase the time it takes to get access, and we reduce the response time. We then buy another mainframe computer and immediately start an educational process that will make certain that the new system will degenerate, just as the old one did.

The only way we can make a time-sharing system work is by restricting users, and this is an inappropriate action for a university to take. This condition has always been troublesome for universities. We do need a computer system and, although a time-sharing system is not the answer, neither is a collection of personal workstations that are not in any sense connected to each other. What we now have within our reach is a solution. It is a network of personal workstations, that is a distributed system that will be connected so that the cohesiveness of the campus can be increased by this distributed system; a system where you can have transfer files and to which everyone will have access, either through public clusters or through personal workstations. There is no question that, over time, almost every student will have a personal workstation.

At Carnegie-Mellon, in working toward this end—a personal computer for every student—we have been able to help, with a grant from the Carnegie Corporation, to organize a consortium of universities. That consortium has defined the requirements for the workstation for the future. It is a workstation that resembles the recently announced IBM PC RT, except the price should be $3,000 or less. There are now several vendors who believe they can meet this set of requirements—including the price requirement—although no one is quite promising the $3,000 price for fall 1986.

So the new computer system that I think is part of this revolution is a network of personal workstations that will (1) be widely distributed, (2) have the capability to plug into the system from dorms and classrooms, (3) be part of a network with the library, (4) be tied together into the mainframe, if there is a continuation of a mainframe computer center or if there is a supercomputer, and (5) be completely tied together to form a computer system that is an alternative to a time-sharing system.

Personal Workstations in Education

The second part of the revolution is making this kind of system work for us in achieving our educational objectives. It is my belief that, with this kind of a computer system and with a network of personal workstations, we can have a major impact on education. It's going to require massive funding for software and it's going to require the same kind of standardization that we have with textbooks.

Standardization of software is something else the consortium has been able to move forward, with the objective that software developed at one university be applicable in other places so that time is not wasted in reinventing the wheel. This characteristic is critical for us. But we also have to standardize the operating systems and the kinds of languages that are going to be used for the software that will be developed. We have been spending something over $1 million a year for software for several years. It probably should have been $2 million, but $1 million was all we could manage. With that investment, we have been able to make a good start on what we can accomplish in this revolution. (Shortly, I will give you a brief description of some of the kinds of programs that I hope will establish my assertion that this is a revolution.)

Increased Student Comprehension

I believe computers can have a major impact on education, but to date the surface has only been scratched. I see three ways that computers can make a major impact. The first is through deeper comprehension. I believe that, with the proper programs, we can, either in the same amount of time we have now or in an even shorter time, develop in our students deeper comprehension than they now achieve. I say this for two reasons, and there are undoubtedly more.

One reason is that the problems we can present to students for solution are problems that can readily be transferred to the real world; that is, we can use real-world problems to test the transfer of knowledge that comes out of the classroom. I don't mean that we don't want the kinds of exercises that you find after each chapter in a math book, but we also want problems that will help students to develop the ability to transfer knowledge to a wider range of areas. For example, students who know calculus must be familiar with many applications from engineering and science so that they can, by understanding the concepts, transfer that knowledge to another field, such as economics. The development of this ability to transfer knowledge requires more and different kinds of problems, real-world problems, that can be addressed with large databases and with other kinds of activities. As another example, with one of the applications I will show you, it is possible for architecture students to learn more about construction through the use of the proper programs on a computer than they are likely to learn now in their course work.

The second reason is that, with the kinds of graphics capacity we are trying to get into these workstations and that are already present in many workstations, we can demonstrate concepts that, in the past, students could only attempt to visualize and try, in their imaginations, to understand. It is now possible, particularly for things like dynamic systems, to show before a student's eyes what is happening in these systems. I believe that this ability to demonstrate concepts will also lead to deeper comprehension by students. I think we can give the students a greater ability to use knowledge. In other words, much of what we do now, particularly in certain areas in the humanities, is teach a student about a subject. I think with the computer, used properly with appropriate programs, we can teach students how to use that knowledge so that, even in a field like history, freshman and sophomore students would be able to "do" history, rather than just to learn about history. This ability is going to increase the level of education that we are able to give students. I think here of an example from the *cahiers* of the French Revolution, which are now on computer and which ten years ago were accessible only to a small, elite group of French historians. Now we can give difficult and complicated questions about the French Revolution to freshman and sophomore students that they themselves can investigate with these data. There are many examples of this kind today. With simulations and with databases in many fields, we can give our students a greater ability to use knowledge.

"Intelligent Tutoring"

The second major impact of computers in education (and in many ways it might be the most important, although it is only beginning) is that we can improve teaching through programs now being developed that we might call "intelligent tutors." In a sense, the programs are expert systems in which the "experts" being simulated are expert teachers. There are several programs that have these characteristics. They are developments from the cognitive psychologists, who are closely allied with the field of artificial intelligence. They have developed programs into which they have built greater knowledge about the way students learn, and these programs can make adjustments in the way they teach on the basis of the way the student is learning in the process of using the program.

With intelligent tutors we are using the cognitive psychologist's knowledge of learning theory, knowledge that is not widespread in academia. Most people who are teaching have, as you know, no training for teaching. Presumably, they know their fields and are therefore good teachers. We know that is false. With intelligent tutors we get a real effort to embed knowledge that would have been good for all of us to have had and to have used as we taught, but which few of us possessed. This is a huge step.

We don't claim to have a lot of solid data on the impact of intelligent tutors, and I don't say that what we have is significant in any sense because we have only a small sample. Nevertheless, there is at least some evidence of much faster learning through the use of intelligent tutors. In one case, there is a belief that material can be taught in roughly half the time it takes with a regular classroom presentation; in another case, dealing with the teaching of geometry to high school students, there is evidence that the students are learning better. It is a tentative, small sample, but there is some evidence the students are raising their grade levels by one full grade. This was a case where the computer came on in the second semester and where certain students were selected. It was presumably a good sample and a well-designed experiment.

Expanded Self-learning Ability

The third major impact of this revolution is that we can give our students greater ability to learn on their own. Through the computer and the kinds of programs we are talking about, our students will truly learn how to learn. One of the terrible things about American education is that we are all in the classroom so long that we come to believe that the only real learning that takes place is in the classroom. I've had professional economists apologize for their mathematics by saying that they learned it on their own—as though there were any other way to learn. But because we are so used to "teaching" in the classroom, we tend to forget that the really critical thing about education is learning how to learn. I believe that when students can take programs of the kind we have been talking about and study these programs by themselves or in groups, they are going to learn how to learn in a much more effective way than is now the case.

One of the good things about this approach is that all fields are included. For a while, people thought that the computer was fine for engineering and the sciences but not for the humanities or the fine arts. This is just plain false. At Carnegie-Mellon, the humanities are, if anything, in the forefront. We now have about 120 different programs that have been developed for all colleges and almost every department.

Examples of New Programs

To give you a flavor of what is possible and what is happening, I would like to read some brief program descriptions or excerpts from program descriptions. This one, in history, is a game called "Go for Baroque." It is a game for analyzing social, political, and economic factors in sectarian strife during the baroque period in Europe. It is a computer game in which:

> the objective is to make students in European history aware of the forces affecting religious affiliation during this period. The program asks them to play the roles of Jesuit, Calvinist and Anabaptist missionaries who must make decisions about which European cities they should visit in order to make converts, weighing the risks of failure, arrest and execution against the gains of conversion. The period in which the game is currently set is Europe of 1615, three years before the last great sectarian war in Europe, the 30-Years War, when the frontier of religious proselytizing moved northward and eastward.

I won't tell you how the game goes; I don't want to spoil it when you want to use it.

There is a program for a course in first-order logic that is a proof-checker and argument-reconstruction environment. It's been used in the classroom, and the faculty member using it reports that the course, which normally takes a full semester to teach, was taught in two-thirds of a semester. In student evaluations of this freshman course, the computer program was most often cited as best feature of the course, and it was least often cited as the worst feature. It received an effectiveness rating of 4.2 on a 5-point scale.

There is a program in psychology called the LISP tutor:

> LISP is an example of intelligent tutoring designed to provide students with private tutoring in learning the LISP programming language, which is one of the main programming languages of artificial intelligence. The underlying goals of the design of the LISP tutor are to provide a friendly working environment for the student as if he were using a smart, structured editor; to provide helpful information that guides the student back to a correct path if he makes a planning or coding error; to represent the conceptual structure of programming better than a simple screen editor.
>
> As soon as the student makes a mistake, the tutor responds with an appropriate diagnostic message. Because a student can write his code a small piece at a time, the feedback appears as soon as the tutor finds that the student is having difficulty coding a problem. It takes him from the coding mode into the planning mode; that is, the tutor works through an algorithm step by step, using an example. After the algorithm is constructed, the student can return to coding. The tutor also provides guidance by hinting toward the correct solution if the student is having difficulty. If necessary, the tutor can provide the next small piece of code so that the student can continue, either by the student's request or after he has made the maximum allowable number of errors for that code. As long as the student follows the path leading to the correct solution, the tutor stays in the background.

That's a good example of what we mean by an intelligent tutor. We have a program in electrical engineering called the "Transient Wave Program." It is an educational program that "uses interactive computer graphics to provide students with animations of voltage and current wave forms as they propagate on a transmission line with reflections at both ends." This is an example of a program that gives the student a better notion of what is happening through the use of graphics.

Another electrical engineering program, the "Gauss's Law Program," is an example of a way we are going to improve conception and comprehension. "It is designed to give the user a better understanding of Gauss's law, which states that any surface integral of electric flux is proportional to the net charge enclosed by that surface. This program allows the user to specify certain things and then watch the integration right on the screen to verify that Gauss's law holds true for each case." This is the kind of thing I mean when I talk about deeper comprehension.

We have a program in music called "Vivace" that:

models, as closely as possible, the human approach to writing music. Vivace's current task is to compose a four-part 18th-century chorale using all the guidelines and constraints needed to ensure good voice leading, preferred doubling, effective choice of chord functions, convincing cadences and judicious use of non-harmonic tones.

The purpose of developing this program was to define more clearly the meta-rules governing the compositional process. Through it, Marilyn Thomas, who developed the program, believes she can teach composition much better in the classroom and enable the student to gain new insights. As she says, it is providing the author with new insights into the decision-making process in writing good chorales. Results of this research have been incorporated into the author's method of teaching students.

In biology there is a program for genetics. One in civil engineering (this is the one in architecture that I referred to earlier) has as its primary aim the creation of "a graphics-based environment in which students can synthesize, analyze and evaluate structural systems for buildings."

I cite these programs simply to give you some notion of why I am enthusiastic and why I say there is a real revolution under way in higher education.

I believe we have a fantastic opportunity with the technology we now have and that the only limitation is our own intelligence.

Computer Technology and the Three Cs of Higher Education

Maurice Glicksman
Brown University

Dr. Glicksman attended Queen's University in Kingston, Ontario, and received his Ph.D. in physics in 1954 from the University of Chicago. He was associated as a research scientist and administrator with RCA Laboratories for fifteen years; four of those years were spent as Director of the RCA Research Laboratories, Tokyo. In 1969 he became University Professor and Professor of Engineering at Brown University. Since 1974 he has been Dean of the Graduate School, Provost and Dean of the Faculty; he is now University Professor, Professor of Engineering and Provost. During 1983–84 he was Visiting Scientist in the Department of Physics at MIT. His research interests have included high-energy physics, plasma physics, and the electronic properties of condensed matter.

W hen we designed this program, our idea was to have a debate
between two persons who would take different sides of the
issues at hand. When I mentioned that to one of my colleagues
at Brown, he said, "Really? I thought both you and Dick Cyert were
technology enthusiasts." I'm not going to say that what Dick has said
is wrong, but I am going to take a different position on the way one goes
about looking at the campus of the future and the role of information
services.

First, I have two concerns that I want to mention. I will come back
to these during my talk. The first is that technology, when it is properly
used in our society, is supposed to serve the goals of society, not the
reverse. Society is not supposed to serve the aims of technology. By the
same token, technology in higher education must serve the goals of
higher education. I believe firmly that modern technology has great
potential for playing a major role in higher education, but I also believe
there is real danger that the opportunity for that role will be squandered
if the approach to the use of technology is to impose it, rather than to
invite it.

One of the problems in dealing with the issue of technology in higher
education—a problem that is not new but that is not often addressed—
is the question of whether we understand why we need technology and
why we want to use it in higher education. A second point, and one that,
having come to an institution of higher education from industry, I am
particularly concerned about, is that there are practically no institutions
of higher education that examine themselves or do significant research
on their own functions; that is, the way they go about education and the
processes they use. There are very fine "institutes" (so named) for
research in higher education at several institutions in this country, but
they tend to deal, not with the more difficult questions of what are we
doing and why are we doing it, but rather with analysis of the outcomes
of what we are doing.

One of the important outcomes that we can derive from our work
with technology, in particular the technology we are talking about, is
an understanding of the impact of that technology on our institutions.
We must understand better how our institutions work and what they
are about. I hope we can encourage more of that kind of thinking and

research in our own institutions as we continue to make use of technology.

I want to talk about the use of technology in institutions of higher education in terms of what I see as the goals of higher education. In this I differ somewhat from the goals described by Dick Cyert. I have divided these goals into three areas: (1) creation of new knowledge, (2) communication of knowledge, and (3) conservation of knowledge. I believe these three are of comparable importance. They intersect each other, but they enable us to define higher education and its aims. I want to say a little about these three goals and about the role technology has played, is playing and, one hopes, will play in the future in improving what higher education can accomplish in these three areas.

Creation of New Knowledge

The creation of knowledge has been part of the tradition of universities for many centuries, and it is often a major goal in universities today. The contribution to new knowledge through scholarship and research by the faculty and students in those universities is also the function most prized by faculty. The faculty in the major institutions and universities think that, when they are contributing to new knowledge, they are carrying out in the best tradition what they see as the goal of a professor or of the faculty. They give the highest honor to those colleagues whom they deem to do best in that pursuit.

Society benefits from the creation of new knowledge at universities, in part because of the use to which that knowledge is put, sometimes by the university itself, sometimes by institutions outside the university. Basic scholarly investigation is done well in universities, and that is one of the reasons that universities (particularly American universities) insist on an open environment, that is, an openness to the sharing of knowledge and an openness to the publication of knowledge, both of which are important in continuing to provide the right environment for creation of knowledge.

Universities design the scholarly and research environment to stimulate the creation of knowledge, and in many cases—I would say in most cases for the major universities—the federal government and foundations have provided major support for this. The students provide support, of course, by helping to pay the bills for the faculty, but the major role in the growth of research and scholarship in universities, particularly since World War II, has been a major influx of funding from the federal government. The reason for this influx is that there seems to be a societal good from the development and encouragement of the creation of knowledge.

What has technology done in this regard? From the point of view of computers and computing, scientific research has undergone major change in the last three to four decades. The efficiency of experimental work has been enhanced by orders of magnitude in some cases; for example, in the ability to get rapid feedback and thereby to control experiments as they are being conducted in many different fields, whether physics, chemistry, or psychology. It has made possible the ability to deal with problems that were hopelessly impractical without technology. The sciences of physics, chemistry, psychology, biology, medicine and geology, as well as a number of others, have all been to a great extent changed by the use of computers for both theoretical and experimental work, and they continue to be changed. This is natural. Change is a phenomenon that is always present, but it has become more prevalent—virtually ubiquitous—as technology has improved.

I would also like to point out that, in great measure, this change has been the result of the response by scientists to technology and their utilization of it in their work. They have actively looked for what is available and for ways to use it. This has, of course, produced a number of by-products. Older faculty have either retrained or have not been retained. They have made use of post doctoral students and technicians to maintain technology-based experimental or theoretical programs. There is no question that peer pressure has forced many faculty members, not merely to acknowledge the existence of useful technology, but to respond actively and positively to it. Not to do so would be an indication that they were no longer productively at the leading edge of their discipline.

The impact of technology has not been restricted to the sciences. It has moved into the social sciences and the humanities, as well. Here, I am talking about research and not about instruction, although it fits both. Computers enable scholars in the humanities to deal with text and textual problems that were intractable in the same way that theoretical problems were intractable to theoretical physicists or chemists before the availability of computers. They have been helpful in library research and in interconnections and correlations that are necessary to deal with tremendous volumes of information that an individual could not otherwise deal with in her or his own way.

In the arts, we are dealing with music, not just in the instruction mode, but also in the composition mode and in the analysis of musical text. We have also seen the creation of at least one new discipline, computer science, which developed from the technology of the use of computers. There is also cognitive science, although I don't know whether I would say that it came from that same technology. Cognitive science comes more from psychology, but the availability of the technology has made a difference in its being able to establish itself as a discipline.

I want to stress that the key factor in this is that the utilization of technology is a result of opportunities and needs perceived by scholars and the availability to scholars of the technology they wanted to make use of. It is a response to a problem; the answer to some needs seen by them. In some cases, although it was not forced, the use of technology was "facilitated." For example, there have been National Science Foundation grants that offered money, thereby encouraging more rapid utilization of technology in certain areas. There are institutional commitments that have helped in this regard, whether they are commitments to supercomputers for research or to the broad distribution of scholar's workstations to enable faculty to make use of them in their work.

Communication of Knowledge

Let me turn to my second goal for higher education: the communication of knowledge, communication of both new knowledge and of information from the past. As I said earlier, universities have a strong commitment to the communication of ideas, information, and knowledge. I would divide the major functions of communications into two parts: the communication of knowledge to peers, "knowledge peers," one might say, and the communication of knowledge to those who could become knowledge peers; vis-à-vis, students, both on and off campus. Instruction is one process in the communication of knowledge; publishing is another. The key societal contribution of the communication of knowledge is the education of society. Communication of knowledge also has an impact, of course, on the creation of knowledge, for communication among peers enhances the effectiveness of research and scholarly work. But its key contribution is educating the women and men of the future to be productive members of society.

What has technology done to advance scholarly communication? It has been important, of course, in communication in the technical sense; that is, the communication of information, or the flow of information, through telephone lines or through the airwaves among computers. Networks are very important and have played a significant role in that kind of communication. Electronic publication has made communication among peers easier. It has enabled more rapid dissemination of information and has improved access to information. Again, these communication links—publication, for example, or electronic networks—have come into being in response to needs perceived by faculty and scholars.

Let me deal, for a moment, with another function of communication: teaching. Technology has not had a major impact on teaching. I respect and appreciate what Dick Cyert said about model courses, and I found his examples of courses being offered at Carnegie-Mellon fascinating, but Carnegie-Mellon may be an exception. The hard fact is that, despite the great amount of effort that has gone into the use of computer technology for teaching, the number of courses utilizing computer technology is still a small fraction of the total body of courses being taught, and the impact of computer technology on the teaching function remains minimal. Most instruction is still by lecture, with blackboard, chalk, textbooks and speech as its "technology." Video, much touted when it was introduced, had very little impact in the classroom, even in its heyday, although it may be making a comeback, now that it can be transmitted over networks. I believe it will some day achieve a more important role, particularly in connection with computing technology.

Many faculty are "Reluctant Dragons" when it comes to the use of technology in the classroom. I don't find this surprising. I believe they probably ought to be. Although faculty are a conservative group (I use the term with a small "c") in terms of the use of instruction, they are also a highly individualized group. Dick Cyert alluded to the assertion that, in essence, the only requirements one must satisfy to come into the classroom and teach in a university are the Ph.D. and publication of sufficient quantity to impress your peers that you have been successful. I think that is an accurate statement, but I do not think it is a satisfactory situation. It is, however, widely held by our faculty colleagues that, in fact, the person best able to determine how she or he should teach is the person who does the teaching. The faculty at Brown, and I do not think we are unique in this, hold themselves and each other in high esteem because of their teaching abilities. They believe that they do not repeat to their students what a textbook has said, that they do not teach the same syllabus or the same way every time they repeat a course. They feel that they put their own stamp on the material and the way they provide the material to their students. As you might suspect, most of our faculty have no desire to change their teaching approach, and in considering the use of technology in the instruction process, we must deal with that in the background. It is my hope that we can change, or improve, the approach but not change the person. I do not believe that the interaction between the individual instructor and the student, in whatever setting it is, is an unimportant factor in the communication of ideas and understanding. This interaction, therefore, is something we don't want to damage or destroy in the process of trying to help with the instructional process.

Let me say a little bit more about the instructional process. I think that the way instruction will take advantage of these new educational tools is through the individual instructors' use of such tools as are available to improve what they, themselves, see as the problems they have in their teaching. This could include all kinds of courses and all levels of courses, from the kind of elementary programming I did teaching introductory statics and dynamics fifteen years ago to giving exercises for the students to play with on their computers so that, as Dick Cyert described, they could see the effects of various parameters in the equations of motion, they could determine collisions, they could deal with gravity and such matters and see the results immediately. That is a good mode of communicating ideas to students, and that mode is embraced by those faculty who see it as being effective in what they want to do.

We are developing on the Brown campus, and I think this is true of many campuses, a growing cadre of persons who are seeking ways to use these tools to improve their instructional approach, just as we have had over the last three decades a growing cadre of individuals in the sciences who use these tools to make better laboratories. I remember going into the Rockefeller University Laboratory twenty years ago and watching psychological experiments on animals being done by computers. There was instant feedback, as well as instant analysis of the results. That process has been going on in scholarship and research and that process will go on in instruction.

There is one area of instruction that is facilitated by technology. It is what one of the background papers for this conference cited as "recurring education as a function of universities"; that is, education for individuals who have already passed through a four-year, six-year or nine-year formal program and are in the "world of work" but want to continue their education with some assistance. Educating one's self is very important and tutoring, whether it is by a machine or a person, can help in that process of education. This function, which will be of greater importance in the coming decades, is one that universities ought to pay serious attention to. A number of institutions are using it now, in the case of continuing professional education. For example, many engineering schools and medical schools have formal programs, and the professional schools are expanding their programs. But the humanities and the liberal arts are just as attractive for this recurring educational activity as are the professions. As institutions, we have not done much in this field, although there is a great deal going on in and mostly out of universities in educating individuals who are formally outside of higher education. Eurich reports that about $50 billion a year is being spent on educating adults.

Conservation of Knowledge

The third role of the university is what I call conservation of knowledge, or conservation of information. I see that function vested in two "repositories," if I may use that term. One repository is the members of the university community, faculty and students who have learned and are learning and who retain information and are able to communicate it. While they are alive and consciously able to communicate, they conserve it. If they are unable to communicate it, they have conserved it, but it is not accessible; when they are not around anymore, it is gone.

The second "repository" is of a more formal and more permanent kind. It involves the storage of information in various media, whether it be in print form, on video tape, an audio recording or some other form. We think mainly of the library as the agency to take responsibility for the storage or conservation of information of this kind, and clearly the library's role in conservation is very important in society. The library preserves the past for future use. Without the conservation process, we would go through a new learning process every generation. This would be highly inefficient for society.

In the conservation of knowledge, technology has yielded good results but results that are yet to be fully realized. Manuscripts were at one time a major repository of information; today, books are our major repository. But books will some day not be the major repository of information, although I do not expect that time to come during my lifetime. There will be other media which, because of the density of information they can hold and the easy accessibility to the information contained in them, will provide more effective storage than books.

Many of us of this generation may experience some psychological difficulties in seeing books disappear, or even in thinking that books are disappearing. For example, I sit in my study and look around at the variety of colors and shapes of my books. I take comfort in knowing that I have immediate access to the ideas they contain because I see the titles on the spines. Then I look at the computer, and I plug into it, but it's not so easy to reach the information it contains. The files have simple names, it's true, but they don't have different colors or shapes, and the titles are my own, which means, unfortunately, that they are all cast in the same mold, whereas the titles on the books are cast from the different ideas of many different individuals. But I think technology can get around that. We can change and make more psychologically pleasing the way we store information electronically than is presently the case, especially if we get some people who have an appreciation of esthetics into the process. We may even come to love the shape, the color and the smell of video disks, or optical disks, just as we came to love the shape, the color and the smell of books. Then I think it won't be so hard a job for us to deal with the problem of books disappearing into machines and shrinking to much smaller size.

Technology has made access to information much easier than it was in the past. Space for storing information is much less demanding in its requirement, and there seems to be greater attraction for the notion of cooperation in the storage of information. One of the problems in cooperating in the storage of current information is the psychological one I mentioned. I wrote a paper several years ago urging that libraries join together in full cooperation because no library in any of our institutions was sufficiently rich to own all the material that the faculty and students in that university need. I showed it to several of my colleagues in the humanities who are lovers of libraries, and they all agreed with me that the logic was correct and that they were wholly supportive, but they declared that their next door neighbor was not, because she or he always wanted to have the book on the shelf in the library that was across the road. That's a psychological factor that is clearly avoided when information is in electronic format, because the electronic format is easily available. There is not any real place where one can say it exists because it exists only when it is transmitted. A book can be physically picked up and taken away, but electronic material can be used only when it appears on the screen of your own workstation or when it appears in hard copy as a result of your printing it out on your own printer. Whether it originated in Palo Alto or Edinburgh or Buenos Aires or Cambridge will not affect your ability to use it. In this regard, the economic value of technology for the use of scholars is great, although it still has to be recognized to be realized, and there is still much development to be done.

Conclusion

Let me sum up by saying that I see the use of technology as offering important opportunities to universities and people. Its use must be justified, and that is where there is a semantic, but real, problem among the people and universities. I feel that it is justified in terms of both qualitative and quantitative improvements. We all deal with data on how valuable the technology is, but none of us will say that this data can irrefutably justify what we are doing with the technology. We can say how much it costs, but we have a great deal of difficulty in saying how much it saves. Can we say that it saves in terms of quantitative improvement, or should savings be measured only in terms of the qualitative improvement of what we are doing? There have been major changes in some fields, such as the physical sciences, and there is bright promise of important changes in the humanities, arts and social sciences in helping us in the creative function. There is no question that technology is here, not only to stay but to be integral to the work of many of the scholars and researchers in universities.

In the communication function, technology is making possible what I call in a technical sense personal communication, in particular publication. In the field of instruction the jury is still out. Many of us in universities, myself included, are working hard to spread the use of technology and to make it available to faculty and students because we believe that there is much to be gained. However, I'd like to be able to satisfy, not only my colleagues but myself, that the gain is a visible one, a demonstrable one, and I have two problems in doing that. One is the very basic problem of understanding the instructional process itself.

This brings me back to the comment I made at the beginning of my remarks. For example, we have an institution called IRIS, Institute for Research and Information and Scholarship, and although its purpose is to support the development of the scholar's workstation, it was set up functionally to evaluate—or to try to evaluate—the impact of those workstations on the instructional process, as well as the research process. The evaluation part of that institute is given equal status with the software development going on. It is headed up by an anthropologist, and I think anthropology is probably the right discipline in which to study a societal function like teaching. It is a delicate matter and, in fact, a very difficult one for an institution to study itself, and therefore the best thing seemed to be to have groups from different institutions make the studies. The University of California at Irvine has a group of faculty whom we at Brown have contracted with to study the instructional modes we are using, to look at what we are doing in the classroom, with and without the technology, and to evaluate impacts on both the instructors and the students. By doing this over sufficiently long periods, we can minimize the Hawthorne effect, the attention-getting that occurs when you bring new things into an old process.

The level of commitment to technology by our institutions is high and is growing. I don't think any of us knows what it should be. At Brown we are putting more than 10 percent of our education and general budget into information services; that is, the libraries and centrally supported computing. Considerably more than that is being committed by outside sources, institutional sources and support from the budgets of the individual departments. The prospect is that, if we are to continue to be successful in the use of technology and instruction as well as in research, the cost will go up.

At some point there will be a question as to what fraction of one's resources can or should be put into the application of computing technology in the educational process. My own belief is that the present sharp focus on computing technology is temporary. Not that the technology is going to go away but that it is going to be treated the same way as the telephone or the fact that we have residences or dormitories for students. Those are all costly items, and they are all part of the business of education, but they have become embedded in the process. If the technology is successful, then it, too, will become embedded. Either we won't be able to figure out the cost, or we won't think of the cost in the same terms as we do now because it won't be identifiable in the same way. I hope that will be the case.

I don't think we will be able to move forward to that goal, however, without some answers to the questions I raised relative to the need for technology and the demonstration that the improvement in instruction, as determined by the instructors themselves, can be accomplished by the use of technology.

Brown has set up a number of task forces over the years. There was one in 1978 that made several recommendations, generally good ones. There was one recommendation of that task force that I want to recall at this time. It was that, in an environment of rapidly changing technology, the most valuable advice to be given is "to retain maximum flexibility to respond to changes." I translate that as "hang loose." I think that's still good advice.

An Examination of Faculty and Administrative Knowledge Workers and Their Major Information Support Units

Evelyn Daniel
The University of North Carolina at Chapel Hill

Dr. Daniel has been Dean of the School of Library Science at The University of North Carolina since 1985. Previously, she taught at Syracuse University, the University of Rhode Island, the University of Kentucky, and the University of Maryland where she received her doctorate in Information Science. She has explored a wide range of library and information management settings. Her varied interests are reflected in her publications, recently "Educating the Academic Librarian for a New Role as Information Resources Manager" (*Journal of Academic Librarianship,* January 1986) and "The Library-Information School in Context: The Place of Library/Information Science Education Within Higher Education." (*Library Trends,* Spring 1986).

S earch! Access! Order! Compress! Transform! These are the operations performed on information by students, scholars, managers, and perhaps everyone else. It is the responsibility of those who provide information resources to make these operations as efficient and effective as possible.

Two factors—one hindering, one helping—must be examined by information resource providers. On the one hand, the generation of data, information and knowledge continues to increase at an increasing rate. Is society coping as best it can with the doubling of knowledge output every sixteen years?[1] On the other hand, there is the rapid, even explosive, development of information technology with its power to store, manipulate, and transmit great amounts at even faster speeds with increasingly sophisticated ways of interacting with the user. Can the administration be confident that technology development in the way of hardware, software, and knowledge management tools will keep pace with the expanding knowledge store? Can we devise, not only the hardware and software, the databases and manipulative procedures, but also an appropriate organizational structure to coordinate this mix of people and machines?

This paper will address some current issues in scholarly communication and information management. The first topic will be the fragmented faculty and their investment decisions and how these decisions relate to scholarly productivity. A central problem here is that of integration and creative synthesis. The second topic concerns the information needs of those who manage the university. There are opposing forces to be examined, some of which lead to a hardening of the dividing line between academic and administrative and others which move toward a blurring and softening of that line. Here the role of knowledge workers in our society deserves comment. The final topic concerns the evolving mission of the major information support agencies on campus—the library and the computing center—with their telecommunication linkages. Attention will be drawn to some parallels among human information processing, computer information processing, and library information processing. The central point here is the primary importance of the network—physical, physiological, and social.

The Fragmented Faculty

At one time faculty and university were virtually synonymous, but no longer. Today we think of the university as a highly complex system with multiple and sometimes conflicting goals. The faculty equate with the production subsystem. They form only one part of an increasingly differentiated small city. Many activities only remotely connected to the academic enterprise have a purpose and function in the university *qua* city and compete for resources.

The production subsystem, as we are realizing in the United States, plays a vital role within any organization. If it does not keep pace with advances in marketing and money management, the organization will suffer a loss of competitiveness.

Universities today are strengthening their marketing/recruitment efforts and their development and lobbying activities. The business and finance offices have been thoroughly professionalized. A beginning has been made toward the more efficient operation of the physical plant, the residence halls, and future space planning. Universities have accepted and acted on earlier criticisms pointed at their lack of businesslike practices. Universities are now managed rather than administered. Strategic planning activities are accepted practice, and careful attention is given to any investment decision whether it be a new building, new curriculum, new computer, or new faculty member.

The core of the academic enterprise, however, has not yet undergone a parallel transformation. The delivery of instruction and the production of research are highly labor-intensive activities for which we hold only subjective measures for multiple and often conflicting objectives. Although this fuzziness may be an essential element of the knowledge transfer and production process, it is clear that pressures relating to finance, governance, and accountability impel both administrators and faculty toward more systematic evaluation procedures for faculty.[2] A major assumption behind this current thrust is that more explicit procedures will improve and perhaps increase the output of scholarly knowledge and informed students.

In a parallel effort, exemplified by the institutions represented at this conference, the scholar's workstation concept has emerged. One intent of this thrust is certainly to improve and increase the output of scholarly knowledge and informed students. The new environment, it is expected, will provide the scholar with tools that will enable him/her to become more efficient and more productive.

To understand the impact of these two current developments—the increased emphasis on accountability and the scholar's workstation concept—an examination of faculty characteristics and attitudes may be helpful.

Faculty Characteristics

The role of the faculty has undergone a substantial transformation from the days when faculty and academy were synonymous. From a predominant teaching role, many faculty members now see themselves first as researchers and consultants and second as teachers. In many cases, the faculty member *qua* researcher operates more as a manager who employs a substantial team of workers of various sorts and who commands considerable resources in the way of space and equipment. Coexisting with these academic stars, individual researchers, and consultants are many who tenuously hold to the primacy of the teaching role. They do little research, by personal preference, but now feel devalued for their lack of scholarly productivity and unhappy about their substantially lower salary and status in the academy.

The image of the university as a research institution holds sway today. Faculty evaluations reflect this. In the future, there will doubtless continue to be a stronger emphasis on scholarly productivity, rather than on teaching or service, despite some protest from the student consumer group. The triple-threat faculty member, strong in research, teaching, and service, is rare. The "publish or perish" message was never stronger.

The composition of the faculty has changed. In 1957, for example, when universities were expanding and certain ones were beginning their climb to greatness, the distribution of faculty by ranks was as follows: 19 percent instructors; 35 percent assistant professors; 25 percent associate professors; 21 percent professors—well over half in the two lower ranks. Thirty-five percent were tenured.[3] Twenty years later, the instructor rank had been virtually eliminated and the faculty were concentrated in the upper ranks. Seventy to 80 percent were tenured. Despite some serious attention to reducing the numbers of tenured faculty and full professors, the latest figures for Carnegie Classification Research I universities show 6 percent instructors; 25 percent assistant professors; 20 percent associate professors; 48 percent professors. Seventy-one percent are tenured.[4]

Salaries have also increased, although perhaps not relative to the standard of living, certainly relative to the university's investent—from an average of $7,000 for an associate professor in 1957 to $31,800 today.[5] There are disparities in salaries today as a result of university efforts to hire and retain professors in competitive fields.[6] Fringe benefits which represented 9 percent of salary in 1957 have risen to nearly a quarter of direct salary costs today.

Faculty compensation, adjusted for inflation, reached an all-time peak in 1972–73 following the years of sustained growth for colleges and universities. Not only were compensations high, but status and a privileged position in society were accorded to faculty, as well. Teaching loads that had been generally set at twelve contact hours per week were reduced to six for research universities. Generous sabbatical policies provided more time for contemplation and scholarship. Life was comfortable for a college professor.

And then it all began to change. Economic growth slowed. The heretofore continually increasing rate of enrollment also slowed and began to decline. The spectre of serious enrollment shortages in the 80s was followed by an insistence on more businesslike practices in universities. This contributed to a very different climate for faculty. Faculty who had been catered to and courted began to experience a more demanding administration and an increase in fiduciary responsibility.

Although there may have been many indicators that life was not going on as before, faculty were not accustomed to looking for these signals from their environment. Concomitant with the growth in the number and prestige of the faculty in the preceding years was a corresponding growth in institutional support units. A growing corps of administrative workers was seeking professional status and advocating investments in new kinds of programs and services, often only remotely connected to academic programs and sometimes in competition with them. Athletics, student and alumni organizations, museums, and institutes of various kinds, instructional support centers, chaplains, counselling services, research laboratories, foundations and development offices, theaters, airports, service stations, snack bars and cafeterias, residence halls, telephone companies, credit unions, television studios, radio stations, and newspapers form a partial list of these expanding activities.

The student body had also changed. Although students are rarely docile, they have in the past generally accepted the curriculum authority of the faculty. Following the many consumer movements that swept student bodies in the late 60s was a demand for new and more "relevant" courses and programs of study. However, addition of new faculty to teach new courses is difficult in a climate of retrenchment. Rather, faculty who had been encouraged to develop depth in highly specialized fields were, in some cases, being asked to abandon their specialties and to retrain in new areas to meet the needs of an increasingly market-sensitive university. Mature faculty members find this difficult.

Faculty Attitudes

Faculty have grown accustomed to expanding their curricula, reducing their course loads, and being nurtured by their universities. They have been generally oblivious to the remarkable changes taking place around them, so the changing attitude of the university administration toward them has come as a considerable shock. Faculty, who have always prided themselves on being more liberal than the general population, find it painful to be accused now of being conservative and unwilling to entertain change, even though the proposed changes sometimes threaten, not only their economic well-being, but also their conception of themselves as academics. Faculty who have worked hard to cultivate a narrow specialty now cling to it, insisting on its importance. The ambiguous nature of the academic enterprise makes it difficult to determine whether any specialty, even if no longer attracting students, may not be important in the long run for a well balanced institution.

The rules for attaining tenure and promotion, as noted above, have also shifted. Good teaching may be necessary, but it is not sufficient for promotion and tenure. There are more faculty competing for a small number of sabbaticals. Internal research support is difficult to obtain. Faculty now have to demonstrate research productivity through publication in scholarly journals.[7] External grant support has become of major importance which means that faculty must also acquire skills of proposal writing and grantsmanship.

In the midst of all these changes in the life of the faculty member has come the computer, whether enemy or saviour is yet to be determined. That it will not be neutral is quite clear. That it will be a boon is also generally believed. The impact on present faculty may not be so positive. Those universities that have aggressively pursued the acquisition of this new technology often made the decision to do so without the kind of scholarly discussion and debate that often accompanies decision making within academia. Thus, faculty are now confronting another externally imposed phenomenon with another new set of rules. Further, faculty have begun to perceive (accurately) that this tool is going to affect their teaching and scholarship in profound and still to be revealed ways. Faculty are also uncomfortably aware that many of their present and future students easily surpass them in ability to use the computer.

It is not surprising that a recent Carnegie study found "College faculty are deeply troubled."[8] The study reports a wide sense of lost mobility, diminishing enthusiasm, eroded compensation, conflicting demands, and constraining conditions of professional life. It found increasing segmentation of faculty. Faculty are less heterogeneous and less loyal to their institutions. Junior faculty are often isolated and a widening generation gap exists. There are more part-time faculty. There is increasing fragmentation into narrow academic specialties and increasingly market-driven differentiation in salaries. Despite the fact that "faculty are perhaps inclined to be critical," a frequent observation in academia, it would seem that faculty have indeed undergone substantial and often dysfunctional consequences as a result of some of the changes detailed above.

Perhaps the most difficult aspect of the scholarly life, however, is something else altogether. It is the problem of integration and creative synthesis. The greater fragmentation of academic specialties appears to be an adaptive response to the increase in knowledge. However, as more and more knowledge is produced, the distance to the leading edge of a specialty becomes further away. The specialties begin to spread further apart to accommodate the growth. The faculty must spend more time in acquiring and synthesizing past knowledge. They must also strive for general awareness of more cognate fields that are also specialized. Thus, the faculty not only face changes in the university's environment and its expectations, but also must struggle to cope with the problems caused by an expanding knowledge base and contrive to generate new knowledge to add to the store.

It is dysfunctional to ignore past knowledge. The "dropped baton" phenomenon of losing knowledge once held and, after a long period of living in ignorance, rediscovering it is well documented in medicine.[9] Redundancy in published information has been estimated to be 90 percent or above (for comparison, language communication is about 50 percent redundancy). It is not clear what redundancy rate will produce maximum efficiency and effectiveness of scholarly communication. Goffman comments that it is truly amazing that such enormous advances in the biomedical field have been made based on a report literature that is only 10 percent efficient.[10]

Compression techniques to wring out redundancy are available. One solution to the problem of ever-increasing amounts of information to absorb and integrate involves developing more comprehensive categories of information, "conceptual chunking." A parallel solution for education is the textbook and for the world's libraries, the state-of-the-art review literature which categorizes, organizes, clarifies, and identifies emerging patterns. These coping mechanisms are examples of information compression. Library/information scientists have long worked to establish coping mechanisms that will reduce redundancy and effect compression through indexing, abstracting, extracting, classifying, and systematizing. Automatic sentence parsers and comparative algorithms may also assist in this process.

The researcher needs not just to compress past knowledge, but to assure that important relationships to other bits of knowledge are not missed. Faculty today face greater difficulties than ever before in identifying related information from fields other than their own. The challenge to the information support system to assist the scholar in this process continues to be the focus of major research efforts.

Manfred Kochen comments on the "secret of the network," in describing current theories of brain organization. He notes that a baby is born with a full complement of neurons but that the baby's brain is only two-thirds the weight of an adult brain.[11] Further, as we age, some of our brain cells may decay. Where does the additional weight come from? Apparently it lies in the connecting tissues that grow and surround the neurons. It may be that this neuronic network enables us to acquire knowledge more and more efficiently as we age. On a human level, we learn to learn through making connections, drawing relationships, and building networks. The social challenge is to perform the same operations on the world's recorded knowledge store. Perhaps technological assistance in knowledge compression and network building will be able to keep pace with the faculty member's growing needs in these crucial and difficult areas.

Parenthetically, we may also need to reassess the current emphasis on research above teaching. Teaching is the process of knowledge transmission; it complements knowledge generation in many ways. Good teaching involves information compression, identification of relationships, and creative synthesis. These are also primary skills for the acquisition and generation of new knowledge.

Although many faculty are troubled and there are even stronger than usual expressions of mistrust toward the administration, faculty have generally shown themselves able to devise ways of coping with the stresses they face. Yet they are wary of simplistic solutions. They see conflicts with no clear sense of what an optimal path might be. The teaching and/or research role is troubling. To be a great teacher requires a different orientation than to be a recognized scholar in a particular academic specialty. The differences relate to investment choices. Teaching requires breadth of knowledge, attention to student psychology, delivery skills, etc. One must invest time and effort to become a good teacher. The generation of new knowledge, on the other hand, requires depth, focus, concentration and occasionally, a ruthless disregard for others. This dichotomy is, of course, too strong, as the complementary ties in teaching and research have been pointed out above. However, the point is that there are unresolved conflicts in faculty time-investment choices.

The Computer and the Scholar's Workstation

The use of the computer in the scholar's workstation holds the promise of making time spent in any activity more efficient. To realize this promise, however, will require an investment of another kind. To master the computer as a tool and to devise new ways of teaching and conducting research exploiting its power requires a substantial time commitment, time that may presently be devoted to mastering subject knowledge or to generating new knowledge. Our social pattern has been that "tool learning" is acquired in youth and honed over time. To expect tool learning to take place in midlife changes that pattern and raises a number of research questions relevant to the ease in which certain kinds of learning relate to maturation stages and hence to productivity, however defined. There is another danger. The computer can be an alluring device which may create many amateur programmers out of previously productive scientists.

Faculty dilemmas produce issues for university decision makers. The five information processing operations cited at the beginning of this paper involved searching, accessing, ordering, compressing, and transforming. Are faculty justified in expecting access to the world's total knowledge store? If so, will this not involve designing more sophisticated knowledge networks? Should faculty expect ease of search and timely acquisition to identified information packages, wherever they may be located and at whatever cost it takes to procure them? If not, where and how might boundaries be set? Is it appropriate to provide human and/or machine assistance to faculty in the tasks of ordering, compressing, and transforming information?

The office automation literature contains many examples of the proportionally large amount of capital investment per factory worker compared with that for the office worker. (A general rule of thumb seems to show about a 20:1 differential.) Office activity is portrayed as inefficient, costly, and labor-intensive. The underlying theme is that the same level of investment in the office worker may cause a dramatic increase in productivity equal to that of the worker so enhanced. Results to date have been difficult to assess, however, because of our inability to measure accurately whether any true increases in office productivity occur as a result of automation. The measures are crude and generally simplistic.

The university now faces a similar situation. It had not, to date, supported faculty from the humanities with substantial capital investments of a technical nature. Universities have invested in laboratories, equipment, and instruments for their health science faculties and their science and engineering programs. Not enough, perhaps, but enough so there are significantly different funding formulas for scientific/technical units as compared with the humanities, the professional schools, and many of the social sciences. Professional schools with high equipment needs are often expected to find support from their constituencies. Although the federal government has assisted to some degree in the provision of the capital required through grants, these are often provided on a matching basis (direct or indirect). In the immediate future, the federal investment may be less, unless relevant to the current vogue of government interest in defense-related research.[12] Corporate grants appear to be increasing but are rarely without specific *quid pro quo* expectations.

The scholar's workstation concept will require substantial additional capital and not just for hardware. Businesses have found that custom software costs increase as rapidly as hardware costs fall. The sophisticated kinds of software required for knowledge workers may prove even more costly. Simple software packages may be easy to use but not very helpful. Very sophisticated packages may require a lot of training before realizing their usefulness. Will the faculty member be induced to make the kind of time investment that will pay off through additional (or better) scholarly products? How will the trade-offs be perceived?

The shift from a primary emphasis on teaching to one on research has been accompanied by a shift of faculty allegiance and loyalty from one that has been institution based to one that is discipline based. The number of departments within research universities varies from about fifty to more than a hundred. The greatest insurance lies in the number and identity of their professional schools. More and more, the disciplinary and professional communities have assumed responsibility for setting goals, generating research agenda and marketing it to federal sponsors, establishing standards for faculty performance, and managing societies and refereed journals. The network community may be more meaningful to individual faculty members than are faculty members in other departments on the same campus.[13]

What impact does this shift in loyalty have on the nature of university and faculty coinvestment in the supply and use of new and expensive tools? If the leading universities work to achieve a degree of standardization in their scholars' work tools, will this make it more attractive for faculty to invest the time and energy necessary to use the tools effectively? Standardization as a possible solution may cause problems, such as the premature adoption of a standard in times of rapid change. The price of the corporate world's investment in the university's need may require a commitment to experiment with prototype nonstandard models.

Even if faculty are provided with the most sophisticated information handling tools, even if they are willing to make the necessary investment to use them effectively, there remain problems inherent with the growth of knowledge and the interdisciplinary nature of many of today's research problems. Faculty are wary and more loosely committed to their employing university than ever before. Investment options are expensive. Because of the high threshold for investment—both in money and in level of effort—most universities and faculty will wish to be cautious in commitment. The downside risk is that delay may be more costly still. Leadership involves risk taking. Those who choose the leading edge position will be watched with great interest by those more timid who will follow.

The Administrative Knowledge Worker

The largest growth in university personnel has occurred in administrative workers. Within a systems framework, if the faculty are the production subsystem, then the various administrative units align with the maintenance, adaptive, boundary, and management subsystems. All of these are information processing units. Their activities need to be analyzed in light of the changes in information flow patterns.

The departments dealing with human resources (e.g., personnel, recruitment, admissions and placement, financial aid and other services, alumni records and the development office, collective bargaining units and other association, religious, and community groups) increasingly rely on information technology to perform their tasks. The same is true for those units dealing with financial resources (e.g., budgeting and accounting, sponsored accounting, financial analysis and control, any internally operated receipt supported unit—theaters, athletics and musical events, the bookstore, cafeterias) plus those dealing with physical resources and other aspects of the management and delivery of academic instruction (facilities management, physical plant, classroom management and course scheduling, curriculum and course tracking, catalog production, and the like).

These units employ knowledge workers[14] engaging in the basic information processing functions of collecting, organizing, storing and retrieving data. Higher level officials or middle managers within these units use the data collected and, through the operations of analysis, synthesis, evaluation and interpretation, produce information for decision makers. Many of these activities have been automated or are candidates for automation, but usually in a piecemeal, fragmented, and non-standardized way. (This is not without its advantages if privacy and security are issues, as they must often be when dealing with human and economic information resources.)

Organizations used to manage things and people, and certainly they continue to do so, but today the emphasis has shifted to the management of information. Yet the "thing" orientation remains and is the cause of much of the fragmentation. Just as researchers can have blinders to relevant information in other fields, so administrative workers often concentrate so intently on their particular departmental concerns that they do not see the parallels in other units.

It appears to be a human quality to expand one's domain as one becomes more knowledgeable about it. (A parallel can be drawn to the growth of recorded knowledge and its spreading tendencies.) Administrative specialties arise and workers demand more information to perform their tasks. More information workers and machines are then required to manage these new specialties. Although faculty expansive tendencies usually relate to the central outputs of the University, the administrative units have an indirect and supportive role. Administrative sectors can and do take on a life of their own, sometimes encouraged by the fact that these units command resources and thus the power to support growth. Reducing the numbers of administrative personnel may be just as difficult a process as reducing the numbers of tenured faculty.

What are some of the factors that divide the faculty knowledge worker from the administrative knowledge worker and what are some of the factors that blur the lines between the two? The realization that both are knowledge workers carrying out basic information handling activities supports their similarity. Task orientation divides them.

To generalize, the faculty member is philosophically committed to free and open access to information and holds a questioning stance toward authority of any kind. The administrative worker accepts authority, seeks direction and is trained to observe privacy and security precautions. The faculty member wishes to explore alternatives in the widest sense, often playing intellectually with various possibilities and reluctant to accept any policy or procedure without hedging it with caveats and voluntarism to protect individual options. The administrative worker is aware of deadlines (often casually dismissed as inappropriate external constraints by faculty) and focused on finding solutions. Workflow pressures militate against overly long deliberations on the administrative side. *Satisficing,* to use Herbert Simon's term for selecting the first workable alternative rather than spending the time to search for the best alternative, is the order of the day. Joint administrative and faculty committees are often marked by serious misunderstandings due to differences in orientation.

A move toward increased professionalism for administrative personnel may serve to complicate matters. Education changes people. A more highly educated middle management group will see the world as more complex and may find itself agreeing more closely with academic colleagues. A more professional attitude tends to make people more dependent on the scholarly record. Professional middle managers are similar to academics in their need to consider their work in an objective and comparative way. They also become closer to outside associations and professional societies which now claim allegiance, lessening their institutional ties. These factors lead to more assertive demands and enhanced status for professionalized areas. It may become as difficult to divest an administrative support service as it is to close an academic department or school.

Internal databases will either be, when viewed pessimistically, the major battleground or, when considered optimistically, the common neighborhood for academic and administrative folk. These databases become vital to the integrated functioning of the scholar's workstation concept but are now "owned" by the administrative side of the house. Clearly many of the privacy and security issues are real, but they may be exaggerated in the struggle for control over databases.

As databases, once the "property" of an individual department, become regarded as institutional property, the control over their design and the design of interface mechanisms will require much greater interaction between academic and administrator. As administrative middle managers become dependent on more access and external information sources for the performance of their tasks, this will also create possibilities for more collaboration between academic and administrator. Carefully drawn lines of responsibility and authority may be challenged through required interactions and the blurring of role differentiation.

Based on a longitudinal analysis of the economic growth of the knowledge industry in the U.S., Machlup estimates that about half of the U.S. workforce is engaged in information handling and processing activities.[15] In a recent work, he and Pagan classify knowledge workers into eight levels and estimate the percent of the total number assigned to each level.[16] The first three levels are relevant here.

At the first or physical level, a message is transported unchanged. Machlup's estimate is that about 5 percent of the knowledge workers are engaged in messenger activity. At the second level, the message is transformed by a change in form but not in content. Twenty percent of the information workers are assigned to this category. The third level involves routine processing. Information is reassembled using algorithms, e.g., bookkeeping. Machlup estimates that 25 percent of all the knowledge workers in the U.S. are at level three.

Thus 50 percent of all information work presently performed is at a physical or routine level. All of these operations have the potential of being automated. Probably about the same proportion of the university's knowledge workers fall into these categories. It seems certain that there will be a major impact on employment on every level with the automation of message transfer, form change, and routine processing.

The implications of these changes for the university are substantial. It is clear that changes in information processing and use are occurring on both sides of the campus and that future planning will have to consider a more comprehensive approach to information flows than heretofore. The management of the transition will not be easy. Virtually all the human workers of the university will be involved. The traditional organizational structure of the university seems certain to undergo considerable reshaping. Incremental solutions are the hallmark of the university. A more comprehensive reorganization may be necessary, however.

This section ends a consideration of the two primary worker groups on campus. There are a number of other groups that might be considered. Clearly the students are also affected in major ways but they are excluded from this analysis as they are deemed to be more malleable and, in any event, have more options. Faculty and administrative workers' needs are changing as a result of changes in the patterns of knowledge distribution and use. Faculty attitudes are changing as a result of changing expectations of students. Aspirations are affected by a changing reward structure. It is the faculty and the administrative core who define the university. It is their needs, their attitudes, and aspirations that must take precedence in considering transitions.

There are also a number of external stakeholders whose behavior and desires have an impact on the university. State and federal legislators affect both public and private colleges. Major vendors like IBM and AT&T influence campus decisions. The alumni lay claims of ownership to the university. The community surrounding the university must also be taken into account. All these constituencies have expectations of the university. Although this paper does not and could not include consideration of these elements, university leadership today must, of course, take into account all the human factors along with the economic and technological factors when making decisions that commit the institution on a substantially different path.

Specialized Information Support Units

In the final section of this paper, the two major information support units with their telecommunication links will be examined for ways in which they may help or hinder the management of the university's information flows.

Synergy means the action of two or more things together to achieve an effect of which each is individually incapable. It is the "something more" that teams and individuals seek to create. Kochen suggests a parallel term, *synsophy*,[17] a neologism which substitutes the root *soph* for *erg*, thus replacing the concept for energy or physical work with that of wisdom. Whatever it be called, synergy or synsophy, we must appreciate its importance. Synergy when applied to physical work can be directly measured. It is less easy to measure when applied to intellectual work, but most would attest to its actuality on the basis of common sense and experience.

Information support systems exist to create synergy through bringing together human minds with the records left by other human minds. Lester Asheim speaks of the literature connection that joined Thoreau and Gandhi, two persons far apart in space and time. That connection "generated a spark that cast its light throughout the world."[18] The integration of the two minds created new wisdom. Other examples of synergy as a result of an information transfer connection abound in the university milieu.

Despite the difficulty of measuring synergy in the information sense, we can seek to understand how it arises, how to control it and how to maximize it. Kochen attributes the secret of synergy to the network.[19] He compares the networking functions in the human brain with the networking functions in the social, scientific community. Communication is the vital ingredient and the network is the synergy generator.

There are four human brain functions that are also characteristic of our human information support systems. First, we can observe our own experience and the objects of that experience. In a parallel way, we can go beyond our five senses by devising information support systems to scan the environment and to identify and record what is happening.

Second, we classify our observations and abstract general categories in conceptual form. Again we have created information support systems, automatic and manual, to classify knowledge in standardized ways. The more sophisticated systems can abstract particular elements from the mass of experience and then order that knowledge conceptually in a greatly compressed way.

Third, we can recall encoded experience that is displaced in space and time. The human memory is a powerful tool. Even before the discovery of printing, however, humans had begun to externalize their

memories and to invest them in signs and symbols. Our information support systems today contain vast amounts of recorded experience encoded
in a variety of forms and ways, conceptually organized and stored for
retrieval, such that Thoreau and Gandhi can be connected over time and
space.

The last unique (we think) characteristic of human brain function
is that we can anticipate new and potential experiences we have not
encountered in any prior time. We role play tough negotiations in our
heads before the actual experience. In athletics, one is encouraged to
enlist the power of the mind to image the right actions for the body's
later follow-through. Our information support units assist us in the same
way through simulations and other what-if scenarios, through predic-
tive programs and forecasting methods, through the provision of aids
to strategic planning.

Thus, we use our brain as an internal information system and then
expand the power of the brain through complex external information
systems. The essence of an organization is its information system. These
systems tend to be isomorphic to the institutions they serve. When the
people within an organization share a common purpose and common
standards and when there is an effective communication network, the
result is an efficient, well-integrated organization. The success of the
Roman and British empires is traceable to their having created such an
organization.

The rapid development of technologies has created a new dynamic
of change. Organizations, particularly universities, tend to change very
slowly. Adapting new technology is a constant strain to the current
organizational structure. The need to achieve both responsiveness and
control influences the choice of communication tools and the kinds of
information support units we develop. Decentralized organizations,
exemplified by the academic side of the university, sacrifice control for
responsiveness. Centralized organizations, exemplified by the administrative side of the university, sacrifice responsiveness for control.

It has been suggested that our model for information systems today
is based on a factory model in which information is conceived as a commodity to be provided by the institution.[20] This severely limits our vision
of what information systems can be. Universities may be losing their collective vision of how things ought to be. A shared vision of some ideal
environment is essential for an effective organization. We need to recreate
that vision.

Academics and administrators alike wish to structure a more integrated personal information environment and have been led to believe
that the technology is now available to make it happen. Although the
technology is indeed here now, the current structure gets in the way and
the lack of a collective vision invites internal conflicts.

How can the university reintegrate and reenergize its faculty and
other knowledge workers? What kind of shared purpose can create

synergy? The university has become fragmented. It exists in two major parts and many minor ones brought together only at the highest levels. The two chief information support systems are also fragmented and isolated from one another. Individuals are divided into many diverse and independent roles. There appears to be an overemphasis on control and a lesser emphasis on responsiveness.

The university as a place of learning for students is a recognized and respected social institution. Is it also a place of learning for the faculty? for administrators? for clerical and technical support staff? Is the learning that takes place helped or hindered by university policies? What direction for learning is suggested? How much investment does the university consciously make in new knowledge acquisition by the faculty and administrative brokers? How much should it make?

The adaptive, responsive organization must be a learning organization, transcending and bypassing the bureaucracy. The traditional organization is generally hierarchical, involving many layers of management acting as information store-and-forward nodes. Communication becomes sluggish because of inherent processing and transmission delays and also because owners of data are selective in what they make available. A well-integrated information system is the key to a restructured university that facilitates continuous learning among all its members, is responsive to changing needs in a changing environment, and provides the necessary coordination and control to unify the total. It might be well to explore structural changes for the university's information system.

The Library

An examination of the central information support agencies as they exist today may facilitate discussion of this issue. The library connects faculty and students to documentary sources of information. The library is traditionally organized into two main parts, public services and technical functions. *Public services* are sometimes partially decentralized through branch libraries and/or divided into undergraduate and graduate main libraries; *technical functions* are generally centralized. As university libraries have grown, they have often added a planning office and a personnel office as staff functions. The technical function is sometimes further divided into a support group (materials processing and business) and a resources group (for collection development and bibliographic control). The resources group also has some service responsibility.

The *senior library executive* is designated Director of Libraries or, increasingly in recognition of greater responsibility and centrality of mission, Vice President and University Librarian. The latter title makes the director a general officer of the university and fosters integrated planning with other senior members of the administration.

The *service group* provides front line information and referral services and ready reference assistance. Circulation, interlibrary loan, collection maintenance activities, instruction in the use of the library and its tools, resources and services are also important functions. The service group is often further subdivided into three broad subject groupings: (1) history and humanities, (2) social sciences, and (3) science and technology. Special collections are often geographically decentralized and may include music, fine arts, business and economics as well as chemistry, geology, math/physics, political science, zoology, and the like. Law and health sciences often operate separate library facilities that may or may not be organizationally tied to the university's main library. Documents, maps, microforms, newspapers, nonprint material, photographic services, rare books, and university archives are also specialized subunits of the service group.

The *support group* acquires materials, produces the bibliographic record, processes materials, provides computer and systems services, manages the facility, and provides fiscal control and other business services. The resources group advises and counsels faculty and students for in-depth reference and research assistance, identifies important materials needed in developing collections, and establishes the policies for bibliographic control, authority rules and points of access.

The *personnel office* formulates a manpower plan, develops compensation and staff development plans, administers personnel activities, and recommends personnel policies.

The *planning office* coordinates planning for decentralized units, formulates and controls budgets, develops reports and applications to funding agencies, and participates in regional and national planning. In addition, major planning responsibility for analyzing and designing systems and for the application of computer and automation technology to library functions have been added to this office and have become a significant responsibility.

Division of the library's functions into three major areas—services, resources and support—has enabled the library to differentiate in response to differing campus priorities. Some choose to invest more in user services, some in larger collections, and others in more sophisticated systems of retrieval and information delivery.

As the world has changed, organizational strains in libraries are occurring in all three areas. At the user interface in the service area, there is a need for librarians to work much more closely with research teams to assure a strong interdisciplinary information base for research work. The current pattern places the information burden on the researcher. As databases grow and access mechanisms become more complex, research projects require the expertise of an information officer. This may necessitate a higher level of involvement with the research process on the part of the librarian and also, an organizational arrangement that allows the detachment of personnel to serve on one or several project assignments on a rotating basis.

Students need a stronger introduction to information resources and their use. Although librarians are now offering credit courses in bibliographic instruction, it seems reasonable to expand these courses to provide an understanding of the nature of information, documentary and nondocumentary information sources, and information use in practical problem-solving.

The impact of changing technology is perhaps most apparent in the support group area of the library where automation of circulation, acquisitions, serials control, cataloging and classification is proceeding apace. The university library is connected in sophisticated and symbiotic ways to national cataloging utilities, to national policy-making groups and to other individual libraries in a variety of simple-to-complex relationships. It would be hard to identify any other institution that has achieved the network of cooperative relationships that university libraries have developed over the years.

Although the mainframe library is still an important fixture on each campus and will probably continue to be for a long time to come, it also can be viewed as a switching center connecting users to materials from all over the world. Online catalogs allow increasingly transparent bibliographic access to the world's documentary sources via telephone links to the library's computers. Physical delivery lags behind bibliographic access and is the locus of future effort.

This changing interlinked system has been costly to create economically and is also proving costly in psychological ways for librarians who were educated for one kind of technology and who have had to retrain on the job to comprehend a different kind of technology that has brought with it considerably more complicated organizational forms. Further changes will be required to realize the dream of universal subject access to all documentary sources of information in a way that transcends the container, the language, and the location.

The resources group also has difficult changes to make. The variety of packaging for substantive information has exploded. Information containers come in many varieties. The library is associated with the book, the journal, the document, the microform, and the manuscript. The library has also provided hospitality to nonprint material (an unfortunate term) of great variety, and now increasingly to machine-readable data in both textual and numeric form. The management and development of these collections have involved both hardware and software decisions. Acquisition of any new type of material carries the requirement for user support via trained staff. Decisions have to be made about the level of support required and the proportion of time to be invested in retraining the staff to work with these various information packages. This is especially true, given that the medium and the message interact. Physical access problems, although important, cannot be the sole source of concern.

The resources group must stay abreast of disciplinary shifts and new methods of inquiry. Fields are continually veering off in new directions for their research interests and curricula emphases. New fields are emerging. The materials of scholarship manifest themselves in new forms. More and more materials are available in machine-readable or other high-density storage form, not always compatible with current equipment and methods for accessing them. The tools of scholarship are changing. This is particularly true in the humanities and the professional schools where there is now a greater emphasis on statistical materials and quantitative methods. The overall orientation to research and learning is changing, from one that has been discipline-based to one that is mission-based and oriented toward practical problem-solving.

All these changes underscore the importance of more strategic planning and the need to consider structural questions.

The Computing Center

The library and the computing center have had very different histories and have operated in isolation from one another. It may be useful to look at the typical organizational structure of the computing center to see if parallels can be identified and if issues faced are similar.

In large research universities there are typically two computing centers, one for administrative data processing and one for academic computing. In some, the academic computing center has been further divided into instructional and research groups. Movements to combine the two for greater efficiency have not been very successful in the past, primarily due to the need for stability and for gradual change in the hardware/software environment of the administrative data processing organization as compared to the need for experimentation with leading edge equipment and software in academic computing. Some coordinated structural arrangement that would serve both needs may be developed in the future.

The *administrative data processing unit* is usually the more sophisticated, and usually the larger center. Typical organizational features include an operations group, a systems programming group, a development group, and a database administration group. Many administrative data processing units also include a systems and procedure group. The operations group is concerned with input/output control, monitoring the system, mounting tapes and disks, and sometimes providing first level assistance for users. The systems programming group deals with systems installation and includes the highest level of programmers who work with the operating systems. The development group is responsible for software applications (e.g., library, student information systems, payroll, personnel, accounting, inventory for warehouse, central stores, physical plant, and the traffic office). The database administration group develops schema and maintains data dictionaries. The systems and procedure group assists clientele in work design, measurement and simplification, and in planning for organizational change.

The *academic computing unit*, like administrative data processing, also has an operations group, a systems programming group and a software development and/or product support group. The latter group frequently provides specialized support for particular statistical, database management, or other major applications packages. There is also a user services group which is now assuming greater importance. There is, of recent times, often a microcomputer resources group which mirrors within its organization the same functions as those of the larger computing center, e.g., operations concerns, installation, and software development and support.

Both academic and administrative computing groups are under pressure to establish more user support in the way of "help" desks, information centers, the provision of formal training and of technical writing support for documentation. The microcomputer resources group, long a poor relation and largely ignored by mainframe shops, has assumed major importance and is radically changing the center's orientation. The variety of packaged software options makes choice more difficult and requires more sophisticated knowledge. As is true for the library, formal and informal instruction in the use of systems and software has become more important.

Some of the same stresses and strains we see in the library are also reflected in the computing center. Parallels to the library can be identified in many ways. The importance of information services from the library, from administrative data processing and from the academic computing center for both faculty and administrative workers, cannot be denied. Both the library and the computing centers face enormously increasing costs of operations. Both must rely on their user constituencies to support their need for an ever-larger budgetary slice. Thus, both must be much more visible in the user community and responsive to its wishes.

The Library and the Computing Center

The library and the computing center must now create and maintain an integrated network and determine which services will be supported in-house and which will be referred elsewhere. As the library can no longer be self-sufficient with its mainframe library, neither can the computing center totally on its mainframe computer(s). Computer centers must begin to develop linkages to regional centers and to other individual computer centers for the provision of supercomputing, technical assistance, software, and hardware not supplied on campus. An articulated, integrated network is the key to the kind of sophisticated information service needed for the campus of the future. The issues surrounding these specialized information support agencies for the university concern:

The impact of continued user and use extension. The administrative knowledge workers must be factored in with students and faculty. The rising interdependence with information agencies in the world off campus carries both opportunities and consequences.

The impact of growing user sophistication. The need for worker control over his/her environment through a personal workstation must be recognized and supported by an organizational structure created to nurture the individual user and to allow and support diversity. That this structure will be different from the present configuration must also be recognized and accepted.

The impact of structural change. The two (or three) information support units need integration at some level and a functional reorganization. Administrative structures will need to be analyzed and streamlined. The patterns of instructional delivery will need to be reexamined. Consideration of differential staffing and support of the instructional and research functions will affect faculty and administrative worker assignments and work load.

The impact of the need for greater connectivity. Faculty and administrators will be accessing some of the same types of material. Technical problems of telecommunication linkages are being solved. Questions of how filtering choices will be made, what level of security for sensitive materials will be maintained, and how faculty, students and staff will be linked to one another to yield synergy, are matters yet to be resolved. If the faculty are provided individual options in their scholars' workstations and if they no longer need to go to the library, the computing center, or to meet with groups of people at scheduled times and places, is there a danger that they will become too isolated? There may be a need for integrators (librarians of the future?) who can serve a personal connecting function through awareness of potentially overlapping areas of research and of similarities in methods of inquiry.

It is reasonable to conclude that the computer revolution has barely begun and that, as for the industrial revolution, the social and organizational consequences for the university will be far reaching. This paper has examined some of the consequences for the faculty, the administrative worker and for the structural realignment of the library and the computing center.

Endnotes

1. As the rate of increase is also increasing, the doubling of knowledge will soon take place at intervals shorter than sixteen years. The consequences of a twelve year interval (or ten or eight) on our education system and on our information support systems will be profound and touch every aspect of how we conceive and pass on knowledge.

2. Neal Whitman and Elaine Weiss, *Faculty Evaluation: The Use of Explicit Criteria for Promotion, Retention, and Tenure*, AAHE-ERIC/Higher Education Research Report No. 2, 1982. Washington, D.C.: American Association for Higher Education, 1982.

3. Data from Lewis B. Mayhew, *Surviving the Eighties* (San Francisco: Jossey-Bass, 1979), 227.

4. Reported in *Change* 17 (Sept./Oct. 1985):36. This will be published in Burton R. Clark, *The Intellectual Enterprise: Academic Life on Campus* (New York: Carnegie Foundation, 1986).

5. As reported for the 1985 academic year in *The Chronicle of Higher Education* (March 19, 1986): 1, 25. The figure is somewhat but not significantly higher when considering only doctoral institutions ($34,900).

6. *The Chronicle of Higher Education* (February 26, 1986): 1, 24.

7. This has encouraged vastly more new journals in an obliging attempt to accommodate the need to publish. Moreover, this may be a necessary response to the increase in new knowledge. It puts great pressure on institutions to increase library budgets to acquire and index these new journals.

8. Reported in *Change* 17 (Sept./Oct., 1985):12. This will be published in Jack H. Schuster and Howard R. Bowen, *The American Professor: A National Resource Imperiled* (New York: Oxford University Press, 1986).

9. The phrase "the dropped baton" originates with W. H. Aberdeen, professor emeritus of the Medical School at the State University of New York in Syracuse.

10. Manfred Kochen, "Levels of System Integration." Presentation at University of North Carolina, Chapel Hill School of Library Science, April 4, 1986.

11. Ibid.

12. See, for example, the report of a conference on "What research strategies best serve the national interest in a period of budgetary stress?" *Government-University-Industry Research Roundtable of the National Academy of Sciences, National Academy of Engineering, and the Institute of Medicine* (Washington, D.C.: February 26–27, 1986).

13. Daniel Alpert, "Performance and Paralysis: The Organizational Context of the American Research University," *Journal of Higher Education* 56(May/June 1985): 241–81.

14. The phrase "knowledge-producing personnel" and "knowledge-producing industries," later shortened to knowledge workers and the knowledge industry, is credited to Fritz Machlup in his *The Production and Distribution of Knowledge in the United States* (Princeton, N.J.: Princeton University Press, 1962).

15. Fritz Machlup, *Knowledge, Its Creation, Distribution and Economic Significance* (Princeton, N.J.: Princeton University Press, 1980).

16. Fritz Machlup, *The Economics of Information and Human Capital* (Princeton, N.J.: Princeton University Press, 1984).

17. Kochen, op. cit.

18. Lester Asheim ed., *The Future of the Book* (Chicago: University of Chicago Press, 1955), 105.

19. Kochen, op. cit.

20. Glenn C. Bacon, "Forces Shaping the New Information Paradigm," The Samuel Lazerow Memorial Lectures at the University of Pittsburgh, School of Library and Information Science, 1985. (Pittsburgh, Pa.: University of Pittsburgh, 1985).

The Information Technology Environment of Higher Education

Douglas E. Van Houweling
University of Michigan

Dr. Van Houweling, Vice Provost for Information Technology, is responsible for coordinating and developing the University of Michigan's computing and telecommunications systems which encompass several campuses, colleges, schools, and departments. He came to Michigan from Carnegie-Mellon University where he was Vice Provost for Computing and Planning from 1981 to 1984. Previously, he was Assistant Professor of Government and Director of Academic Computing and Associate Director of Cornell Computer Services at Cornell University. He received his undergraduate degree from Iowa State University and his Ph.D. in government from Indiana University.

In commissioning this paper, Michael McGill, Vice President, OCLC Offices of Research and Technical Planning, asked that it fulfill two purposes. First, it was to "perform a tutorial role" for some of the attendees at the conference on Information Resources for the Campus of the Future. The paper was to "inform the readers of the information resources on campuses and how those resources are changing." Second, the paper was "to raise issues that will be the basis for discussion among conference participants."

This paper, despite its considerable length, probably does not fulfill either of the purposes. Nonetheless, the reader may find it useful to have some guidance on how to read the paper. The main "tutorial" elements of the paper are in the "Technology" section. Even in that section, I have undoubtedly made statements that may occasion discussion at the meeting. The rest of the paper is devoted to policy issues. Most of those policy issues are nontechnological even if driven by technology. The technology policy is concentrated in the section entitled "Systems Architecture for Higher Education."

The paper focuses heavily on the technological issues surrounding information and its use in higher education, but many of its propositions are organizational and strategic. I look forward to discussing some of the issues with you at Wingspread.

Introduction

Higher education in the United States encompasses objectives that range from helping young people mature to advancing frontiers of knowledge. All of these objectives rest on the ability to create, transmit, store, and use information. In recognition of information's central role in the university's mission, the symbolic center of every major university historically has been the university library. Over the past twenty years, those libraries have become increasingly dependent on new technologies for the management of their information resource and are now beginning to use even newer technologies in support of the delivery of information.

In parallel, a new central activity has grown, usually from modest beginnings in a small scientific or statistical laboratory to a large organization with a budget rivaling that of the library. These organizations, variously known as computing centers, computation centers, computing services, or, in some cases, as information technology services or information resources departments, have been moving steadily from a focus on the manipulation of numeric information to a broad role that encompasses information in all of its forms. At most major universities, the library and the information technology organization have begun to work together—albeit sometimes in an uneasy or even competitive relationship.

In the resulting rapidly changing environment, this paper will:

1. Explore information technology, its recent history, and near future,

2. Outline the impact of the technology on information and its use within institutions of higher education,

3. Describe a systems architecture for the future of higher education,

4. Examine some of the organizational implications of the technology and its use, and

5. Assess the future prospects for the use of technology to support information processing in higher education.

The paper is by no means a work of science fiction, since the technology base to realize its projections now exists. Nonetheless, it has been written at least partially to encourage examination of the implications of the present and future interaction between information and technology. While it is impossible to be confident that the futures outlined here will be realized, it is easy to be sure that the actual future will be at least as different from the present. In the final analysis, then, this paper is about technology change and its impact on academia. The paper should stimulate discussion not only regarding the prognoses it makes, but also regarding other probable scenarios with equally important implications for higher education and research.

Information Technology Strategy

Information creation and dissemination is fundamental to the research and teaching missions of higher education. As information technology becomes increasingly useful, a clear understanding of institutional strategy regarding technological support for information processing has become imperative. Universities need more in their libraries and computing centers than a competent staff providing high quality services. The rapid change taking place in the underlying technology means that high quality execution may do more harm than good. As Drucker observed, doing things right is not enough. "The pertinent question is not how to do things right, but how to find the right things to do and to concentrate resources and efforts on them."[1] A clear view of the future is essential to avoid heavy investment in technology and organizational forms that may soon be obsolete.

A strategic view is not only important to guide decisions, but also to generate cooperative effort. Higher education is governed and administered in a decentralized, bottom-up fashion. As a result, the vitality of higher education depends enormously on the wisdom of literally thousands of decisions made every day by the essentially independent agents that comprise the university. If the faculty, staff, and leadership are to use the capabilities of information technology to best advantage, they need to share an understanding of their institution's strategic course. Consensus on that broad strategy enables institutionally rational decentralized decisions.

In other words, a strategic plan not only determines the foci for concentrating resources and efforts, but also provides a "story" outlining the institution's information technology directions. That story is, in turn, a fundamental requirement for the very concentration of resources and efforts needed to realize the desired outcome.

For instance, major initiatives in information technology usually require resources beyond those in the institution's existing base. A corporation or legislature is unlikely to provide additional resources unless it understands the role that support will play and what broad objectives it will enable. Also, as the required investment in information technology increases, its budgetary impact cannot be defended simply on the basis of the growth of the traditional activities and organizations. The president, central administration, and deans all need to understand and subscribe to an information technology strategy before they can decide to support the required investment and defend that investment against competing resource demands.

An institutional strategy for information technology must be built on technological forecasts, be responsive to institutional needs, and anticipate the opportunities for use of technology to meet those needs. The strategy can then outline the architecture for the information technology environment, the organizational forms required to support institutional use of information technology, and support planning for change in scholarship and instruction.

The Coming Convergence

The convergence of university library operations and the university's computing resources is already becoming obvious at most universities.

At Columbia University the director of the library system has also become the director of the central computing resource. As an increasing proportion of the information used in higher education is represented in digital form, this trend should extend to a steadily broader set of activities. For instance, a number of universities have now begun to integrate their overall communications infrastructure with computing. This partially results from the fact that modern telephone systems are themselves based on large special-purpose computers. More important, this convergence is a result of the increasing need for high quality data communications and the synergy that can be obtained by coordinating voice and data communications facilities.

Few universities, however, so far have taken the further step of analyzing the potential role of information technology in information distribution. Little consideration has been given to the need for effective interfaces with the campus mail system, both internal and external; with the duplicating and printing operations at the departmental and all-university level; and with the university press with its impact on scholarly communication. All of these traditionally, "low technology" services will provide important points of opportunity for effective use of modern information technology. As a result, our budgetary and organizational planning will need to appropriately assess the role that each of these organizations plays in the future of the university.

Technology

Technology or its absence has determined patterns of human information use over the centuries. From the dyes used to create the first cave paintings, to Egyptian papyrus, Gutenberg's printing press, the photocopying machine, and the word processor, the availability of technology has formed the foundation for creation, storage, transmission, and use of information. Digital computing technology is now having a massive impact on information processing.

The very word *computer* is increasingly becoming an anachronism. A steadily smaller proportion of the installed "computing" power is being used to compute numeric solutions. In other words, "computers" are not being used any longer primarily to do "computing." "Computing" technology's potential impact will therefore increasingly result from nonnumeric applications. As a consequence, this paper embraces the past, the present, and the future in a more comprehensive category called "information technology."

The noncomputational use of information technology results from the capability to represent all types of information in digital format. All information, whether it be images, speech, music, diagrams, or the written word, can first be translated into a string of numbers and stored, processed, and/or transmitted in that form. At the other end of the process, those same numbers can be interpreted to recreate information in the form that it was originally expressed. Since computers are able to manipulate digitized information, advances in computer technology are now being applied to information of all types.

While information technology, of course, includes the myriad machines we use to produce, store, transmit, and use information, I will focus on the new information technology made possible through electronics and based on digitization of information. That technology can be divided into categories of hardware and software—the equipment that physically embodies the technology and the content that is delivered by that hardware. These two categories of information technology combine to create capabilities by which human beings can use information technology.

Hardware Information Technology

The machines we have come to know as computers are the product of the electronics revolution. While computers were created many years ago by combining mechanical elements, none of those machines were able to carry out a procedure of any substantial complexity without direct and continuous human intervention. All of this changed in the early 1940s when the first electronic computers were created using vacuum tubes. Vacuum tubes were bulky, consumed large amounts of power, gave off large amounts of heat, and were relatively unreliable. The price-performance ratio of vacuum tube computers was therefore comparatively poor. Nonetheless, hundreds of vacuum tube computers were built and used primarily to solve numerical problems of scientific, business, and accounting nature.

Starting in 1959, the transistor, an invention of the late 1940s, was sufficiently developed to be used in the construction of computers. The resulting second generation of electronic computers provided an enormous increase in reliability along with a radical decrease in size and power consumption. Suddenly, computers could be made much more powerful and less expensive.

In the late 1960s and early 1970s, a new technology, microelectronics, allowed multiple transistors to be combined into a single circuit element called an integrated circuit. Those circuits were combined to construct a third generation of computers based on integrated circuit technology. All modern information technology uses integrated circuits heavily. As a result, the cost-effectiveness, reliability, and capability of information technology is tied closely to the development of microelectronics and integrated circuitry.

Microelectronics development has provided a tenfold improvement in price-performance every decade since 1950. Cumulatively, the cost-effectiveness of information technology increased a thousandfold between 1950 and 1980. Work now emerging from the development laboratories ensures that this rate of advance will continue for the next decade. Basic research now under way will almost certainly provide the same capabilities for improvement in the following decade or two. By the end of the century, we project a hundred-thousandfold improvement in cost-effectiveness. In other words, information technology that cost $1,000,000 in 1950 will be available in the year 2000 for $10.[2]

Information technology will continue to improve in cost-effectiveness for the foreseeable future at a rate at least comparable with the recent past. This fundamental change is the driving force underlying the information technology revolution.

Computer Hardware

Technological change has led to important changes in the manufacture and sales of computing technology. First and second generation computers were all large machines which required "computer room" environments to meet their power and cooling needs. They cost more than a million dollars, served whole organizations, and became known as "mainframe" computers.

While the third generation of computers also included mainframes, integrated circuitry allowed the development of less expensive computers. In the mid-1960s Digital Equipment Corporation pioneered the development of the minicomputer, which usually cost more than $25,000 and less than $1,000,000. The minicomputer had as much computational capability as the mainframe of five years before, and was widely adopted by departments and research groups to carry out their specialized computational tasks.

As microelectronics advanced, it became possible to fabricate single chips containing tens of thousands of transistors. The culminating development was the microprocessor—a computer on a single chip of silicon. These microcomputers occupy a chip of silicon less than one-quarter of an inch square, and provide more computing capability than a room full of vacuum tube computers could provide in the 1950s. The microprocessor, in combination with other integrated circuits, made it possible to build the microcomputer. Since the microcomputer was inexpensive enough to be dedicated to a single person, it also became known as the personal computer.

Changing scale economies

Until the mid-1970s, the computing industry broadly accepted a formulation developed in the late 1940s by Herbert R. J. Grosch (known as Grosch's Law) concerning economies of scale in computers.[3] He proposed that computing power increases as the square of the cost of the computer, so that, for example, twice the money buys four times the computing power. The obvious response to Grosch's Law was to combine, insofar as possible, all of the money available for computing and acquire one large shared computer. The result was the development of the corporate data center and the university computing center, in which one large machine was purchased to serve the needs of the whole organization.

With the advent of the minicomputer Grosch's Law began to break down. In the early 1970s distributing a number of smaller computers throughout an organization became a more cost-effective solution for some tasks than performing those tasks on a mainframe computer. The advent of the personal computer in the 1980s has completely overturned Grosch's Law. Personal computers now are produced by the hundreds of thousands, allowing low per-unit development costs and mass production economies. Computing power is now considerably less expensive to purchase in the form of many small computers than in the form of one large computer of equal power.

These savings on computing power are offset partially by the lower average level of utilization typical of a small computer, especially one dedicated to a single person, compared to a large shared machine. Even allowing for lower usage levels, however, most organizations have by now accepted the notion that large amounts of computing power should be dispersed throughout the organization via microcomputers, which are dedicated to individuals; and via departmental minicomputers, which provide shared resources at the departmental level; as well as in large mainframe computers, which can accomplish tasks too large for personal computers and minicomputers.

The distribution of computers throughout organizations has combined with the need to share information to place an increasing focus on communications technology.

Communications Technology

Throughout history, communications technology has enormously influenced the way in which human beings use information. Communications "technology" probably started with shoes for messengers—people possessed of fleet foot and good memory. It evolved through the use of various types of signaling, ranging from sound signals to smoke signals. Since about 2000 B.C., however, the dominant approach to precise communication over time and/or distance has been the transmission of a written document. Written communication dominates modern industrial society mainly because it is supported by an impressive set of technologies ranging from the ball-point pen to word processors and printing presses. The microelectronic revolution and digitization now provides the potential for expanding human communications beyond the written document to communication of voice and pictorial information.

Transmission technology

Electricity provided a powerful new potential for communications that was first used along with electromechanical devices to transmit information via telegraph. Shortly thereafter, the telephone was invented to transmit sounds from one location to another. Improvements in electronics technology have subsequently increased the rate of message transmission and the number of separate messages that can be carried concurrently on any particular communications medium. For example, since cost-effectiveness improvements in electronics technology have far outstripped the cost-effectiveness of installed wiring, electronics has been used to greatly increase the message-carrying capacity of copper wire. In the 1960s, 10 characters-per-second was the customary rate of data transmission over telephone lines. Technology is now being installed which allows transmission rates of over 300,000 characters-per-second on standard telephone wiring.

Electronics has also enabled us to make effective use of radio to transmit and receive information. The most striking application is the use of geosynchronous satellites, which are placed in orbit at an altitude of 22,300 miles so as to remain stationary in relationship to a particular point on the earth's surface. The satellites use a solar-powered receiver and transmitter to relay information transmitted from one satellite antenna on the earth to another. Since the total distance covered by the signal is substantially independent of the distance between the two communicating antennas, communication costs via satellite are distance independent.

The cost of information transmission over a distance exceeding 400 miles is therefore no longer dependent on the distance. Indeed, transmitting information from Chicago to San Francisco is no more expensive than transmission from Chicago to Cleveland. A substantial barrier to the collaboration of human beings separated by large geographic distances has therefore been removed.

Another innovation in radio communications, which will become more important in the years ahead, is the use of cellular radio. Cellular radio uses computers to conserve space in the radio spectrum and therefore potentially allows fixed wiring to be replaced as the dominant mode of local information distribution. Continued advances in microelectronics may render cellular communications inexpensive enough to become the dominant form of linkage to individuals in local areas.

Light wave communication on glass optical fibers is likely to dominate future communication of large amounts of information between fixed points over short and medium distances. With fiber-optic communciation, electrical impulses are impressed on a laser beam directed into one end of a thin, transparent glass strand. At the other end of the same fiber, a detector changes the laser light back into a digital signal. A bundle of optical fibers, each about the thickness of a human hair, can transmit thousands of telephone calls or video signals at the same time. Optical fibers are routinely providing hundredfold improvements in cost-effectiveness of communications and are increasingly dominating point-to-point communications.[4]

Communications networking

Information transmission technology is not enough—the transmission facilities must be combined with various types of equipment and integrated to create a network. Without careful attention to network design, communications devices cannot provide useful services. For example, shortly after the telephone was invented, a number of competing telephone companies provided services in major metropolitan areas, but those companies were not interconnected. As a result, communication with a substantial portion of telephone users required telephones from several different companies and knowledge of the people served by each company. The obvious difficulty of use and extra expense engendered by this situation led to the creation of the public communications monopolies that developed the voice communications standards underpinning today's worldwide voice communications network.

Data communications networking is not, however, so advanced. In most commercial enterprises and universities, several different communications networks exist side by side. Full use of the information technology resources therefore requires access to devices connected to each of the networks. The University of Michigan, for instance, has three separate networks. One supports Wang office automation facilities, a second supports IBM mainframe computers for administrative data processing, and a third provides access to the academic computing facilities. While these three networks can now exchange information, such internetwork activity is cumbersome and not yet available to all users. At the same time, a number of additional small networks have sprung up to tie small groups of computers together with minicomputers or other personal computers. Those smaller networks usually are not connected to the campuswide networks. Work is now underway to choose small network solutions that will be compatible with the institutional network environment.

Campuswide network integration will be accomplished by taking advantage of communications standards. The foundation for those standards has been developed by the International Organization for Standardization (ISO) and is known as the *Reference Model for Open Systems Interconnection (OSI)*. The OSI model divides communications into seven different layers, with the physical layer (which defines the way the wiring is arranged and used) at the bottom and the applications layer (which defines the applications using the network) at the top.

At the present time, standards developed by the Institute of Electrical and Electronics Engineers (IEEE) dominate the lowest two layers. The most broadly used of those standards is IEEE 802.3 for Ethernet.[5] However, in just the same way that the existence of the transatlantic telephone allows voices to be transmitted, but does not ensure that the voices will be understood at both ends of the conversation, the existence of these standards allows machines to communicate digital sequences, but does not define the contents of those sequences.

At the next levels in the OSI Model, the network, transport, and session layers, two standards are dominant in higher education. The first is the *Transmission Control Protocol/Intermet Protocol (TCP/IP)* standard that has been developed and promulgated by the Department of Defense through the Advanced Research Projects Agency (ARPA). TCP/IP protocols are the foundation of ARPANET, a networking experiment, and a number of connected networks that together form the TCP/IP INTERMET.[6] These networks form the backbone for data communications in computer science, electrical engineering, and artificial intelligence research in the United States today. Indeed, persons without access to the ARPANET or one of its connected networks are effectively cut off from effective collaboration in these fields because the ARPANET has become so dominant a means of communication in those disciplines.

The upper layers of the ISO standards have become increasingly important in higher education. Because they have the weight of the international standards community behind them, the ISO standards in the long run will probably be adopted for most information transfer. Today they form the basis for communications in most of the commercial networks such as Telenet and TYMNET. The academic library community is also planning to use the ISO standards to network university library systems together.

IBM has created a last set of standards, called *Systems Network Architecture* (SNA), that have been more important to the business community than to higher education. A substantial number of information technology devices built by IBM can communicate only through the SNA networking standards. IBM has recently committed to support of the ISO standards and to migration of the SNA standards to those promulgated by ISO. As a result, SNA will have increasing impact on planning for communications in higher education.

Finally, a number of other manufacturers have developed their own standards. Probably the only one of these that is widely used in higher education is the standard developed by Digital Equipment Corporation in support of Decnet. Digital Equipment Corporation has now provided a means of interfacing Decnet to SNA and ISO networks.

The standards environment is rapidly evolving and standards adherence is steadily improving. Nonetheless, the full interconnection of networks and easy passage of information from a network using one set of standards to a network using another is unlikely to be realized in this decade. Considerable effort will continue to be needed to create coherent information networks both within and among universities. Communications networks will therefore continue to be at the center of the institutional and multi-institutional planning efforts in the community of colleges and universities across the world.

Storage Technology

Information storage prior to the development of electronic computers has been primarily through the use of physical systems such as printing presses, cameras, and phonograph records. This all began to change with the use of magnetism for the storage and retrieval of information.

Magnetic recording

Through the magnetization of some medium, an electronic signal can be recorded for later retrieval. The earliest form of widely used magnetic storage was the wire recorder in which wire was magnetized to store voice and other sound information. That technology soon evolved into tape recording in which information is stored sequentially on a long strip of tape with a magnetic coating.

Information recorded on tape is difficult to access in a random fashion because the tape must be read through from the beginning to the point where the information is stored before the information can be extracted. As a result, magnetic recorders have been developed which arrange information much like it is arranged on a phonograph record. By correct positioning of a read/write head over the surface of magnetic disk, any information on the disk can be accessed within less than a hundredth of a second. The actual form that a magnetic disk takes varies from the simple and inexpensive floppy disk used in many personal computers capable of storing a few hundred thousand characters up to the very large (up to four billion characters) and expensive magnetic disk units attached to large mainframe computers. Magnetic disks have become dominant in the storage and retrieval of digital information.

Optical recording

Over the past five years light waves have become useful in information storage just as they have become useful for communication. The laser video disc player was the first mass consumer use of optical recording technology. The players use a laser to read information from which a television picture is re-created.

More recently, the *compact audio disc (CD)* has become very popular. The compact disc is significant because it records sound in digitized form. The recorded numbers are created by sampling the sound to be recorded approximately forty thousand times per second. The numbers are laser-encoded on a master disc which is then duplicated at relatively low cost. A laser-equipped playback unit reads the duplicate disc and a small computer interprets the resulting stream of numbers so as to re-create the recorded sound. The compact disc is similar to a conventional record in that it is a "read-only," that is, new sounds cannot be recorded on the disc after it is manufactured.

Similar discs are now beginning to be used to store information for use in personal computers. In this form, the discs are known as CD-ROMs (read-only-memory) and have a capacity of 550 million characters. As the read-only-memory part of their designation makes clear, these discs cannot replace magnetic disk storage because the user cannot record additional information. Technological development now underway will probably make optical recording technology usable for both reading and writing within the next few years. We can expect, therefore, to have read/write optical discs with a capacity of a quarter- to a half-billion characters. Disc units will be available in quantity at prices probably not in excess of $500 before the end of the decade. For a number of uses, they may displace magnetic recording technology.

Finally, there is a hybrid technology called *magneto-optical technology* in which laser light is used in combination with magnetic storage technology to reap the benefits of both technologies. The roles magnetic, optical, and magneto-optical recording technology will play in future information technology environment is unclear. The impact of having such large amounts of information available for direct computer processing will be enormous.

Software Information Technology

Developments in computer software, while not so much noticed, have been at least as remarkable as developments in computer hardware. Since hardware must be available before the software can be created, software advances lag hardware development by several years. As a result, the computing hardware that we have access to at any given point in time is not fully used by the available computer software.

The first electronic computers were really large electronic calculators custom designed to carry out a narrow range of tasks. Indeed, the first of them was used to create gunnery tables for the Navy to support the war effort during the 1940s. These early machines had to be rewired when directed at a new problem. They were capable of only a few primitive operations, which included simple arithmetic and ability to input and output numbers. They did perform with comparative accuracy and speed, which made them very useful for routine repetitive tasks.

Stored Program Computers

Computers as we know them today did not really exist until 1945, when John Van Neumann invented the stored program computer. The Van Neumann machine is a computer that interprets numbers stored in its memory as instruction codes that direct its actions. As a consequence, a Van Neumann machine, if appropriately designed, does not need to be rewired to solve a new problem. Instead, all that is necessary is to introduce a new set of numeric codes into its memory locations, which are then interpreted by the computer as instructions for solving its new task.

The concept of the stored program is basic to all of the applications now addressed by information technology. The stored program enables a single computer design to be used to solve thousands of different problems, and it enables solutions that one person creates to be used by other persons. Without a computer program, a computer is useless. The program tells the computing equipment how to interpret, process, store, retrieve, and display information. In short, the computer program or software controls the behavior of the computer.

Types of Software

Software can best be divided into three categories. The first category is called systems software. *Systems software* is usually "bundled" with the computer and provides the basic interface for the computer to carry out tasks. Systems software, for instance, includes the program that links the keyboard and the display to the computer, that provides the format and the capability to record information on and off disks, and that provides the user with a set of commands to instruct the computer to execute other programs. The second category, *tool software,* supports the creation of new applications programs. The various computer programming languages are good examples of tool software. The third category, *applications software,* consists of the computer programs actually used to process the user's information. Good examples are word processing and accounting programs.

Computer software has been increasingly used to shift work from the human being to the computer. This transformation started with tool software and has continued into the current personal computing environment. The transformation has resulted from increased software capability and has been associated with changes in the form of interaction between the human being and computer.

In the 1950s, all categories of computer software were written by expert programmers who understood in detail how the computer operated and which numeric codes caused the computer to carry out any specific operation. Programs were simply columns of numbers that directed the computer to carry out specific operations on numbers stored at particular locations in the computer.

Computers therefore could be used feasibly only in applications that were repeated thousands of times because the effort required to prepare the computer to solve a problem was so large. Indeed, computers sometimes worked for days at a time on a single repetitive problem. Convenient and powerful software was required before computers could be used for shorter and smaller problems.

The evolution of systems software

The first innovation in systems software, *the batch operating system,* focused on increasing the efficiency of computer operation. This systems software allowed the computer to sequence rapidly from one small job to another. As a consequence, batch operating systems allowed literally thousands of users to submit their problems to the computer for sequential execution. The user submitted the problem to the computer (usually on punched cards) and came back minutes or hours later to retrieve the results.

As the computer became more powerful and cost-effective, maximizing computer efficiency became less important than achieving greater user efficiency. As a result, time-sharing operating systems were developed to allow hundreds of users simultaneous access to the computer.

Time-sharing systems maintain the illusion of simultaneous access by rapidly switching the computer's attention from one user to the next until all users wishing attention have been serviced. While such switching places a substantial burden on the computer, the resulting interaction between the user and the computer can be made conversational. Rather than submitting a job and waiting several hours for response, the user enters a keyboard command and the computer responds to that command immediately. As a result, the user can examine a response before entering the next command.

Interactive computing (sometimes also known as time-sharing) became the dominant mode of computing in many universities during the 70s and is still used widely in the 80s. The advent of the personal computer and the new economies of computing hardware have made it possible to dedicate a computer to each user. Interactive computing is now provided less and less by large time-shared computers, and more and more through the deployment of many thousands of small computers. Those small computers also have operating systems, such as Microsoft's MS/DOS and Apple's Finder for the Macintosh, which are designed to facilitate interactions between computer and user.

Tool software

At the same time that software was evolving to facilitate human-computer interaction, computer programs were written to facilitate the creation of other computer programs. The first tool software, called an *assembler,* substituted alphabetic names for the operations the computer could perform and for the storage location upon which the operation was to be performed.

Shortly thereafter computer programs called *compilers* were created that translated short declarative sentences written in a highly stylized form of mathematics and English into a computer program. The first such compiler was called FORTRAN for FORmula TRANslation. Since then, a number of compilers have been developed for other computer languages that include COBOL, PL/1, PASCAL, LISP, and Ada.

All of these tools require that the programmer describe in detail each step that the computer needs to take to solve a particular problem. As a result, these languages are called *procedural languages* because they express the steps through which the computer must go to reach an outcome. The computing power made available through microelectronics led, in the early 1980s, to the development of a new type of computing language, that is, the nonprocedural language.

Applications software and nonprocedural languages

Nonprocedural languages form the basis for most applications software. They became especially popular when the development of personal computers allowed a very significant amount of computing power to be dedicated to a person. Nonprocedural languages often do not seem to be computing languages in the traditional sense. The primary benefit of a nonprocedural language results from the modest user expertise concerning computing required for successful application.

The most broadly used is undoubtedly the *electronic spreadsheet*. By placing formulas and numbers in various cells of a matrix, a user can create a large information storage and processing structure for problem analysis. The electronic spreadsheet has applications ranging from accounting and planning to solving differential equations. The key to the spreadsheet is that the user does not have to tell the computer how to solve the problem but rather expresses the problem to the computer in a stylized form. The computer itself produces the solution.

The boundary between tool and applications software is blurred by some nonprocedural languages. Many people would think of an electronic spreadsheet program such as Lotus 1-2-3 as an applications software package. Lotus is also tool software because programs can be written using Lotus 1-2-3 macros. As a result, Lotus 1-2-3 is sometimes used as a tool to develop new applications and sometimes used simply as an application to process information.

There are a number of other nonprocedural languages available. Some of the first were developed for social scientists in support of statistical processing. Today, a number of nonprocedural languages support the definition, creation, use, and retrieval of information from computer databases.

Technology and Human-Computer Interaction

All three levels of software, systems software, tool software, and applications software, are now being combined in new and creative ways to support the user in problem solving, not just of a numeric nature, but also problem solving across the full range of information.

Interactive computing using a personal computer provides a new set of opportunities for the interaction between the user and the computer. In particular, since the communication lines between the computer and the output device (usually a televisionlike display) have become so short, very large quantities of information can be economically moved between the computer and display. Such a close coupling of the display to the computer, while possible with time-sharing computers, was discouraged by the cost of providing the required high-speed, long distance communications link. As a result, the personal computer user can interact more closely with the computer.

In fact, the use of a rapidly changing graphics display enables many of the most popular applications of personal computers today. Among those applications are spreadsheets, word processors and the various drawing and painting programs. Among the most striking recent applications are the tools for creating diagrams and pictures on the personal computer. In particular, the MacDraw package for the Apple Macintosh allows users with little knowledge of the mechanics of drawing to develop charts and diagrams that can be subsequently included in documents.

With appropriate software and hardware, computers can now operate as sophisticated electronic voice-mail systems. The computer is equipped with the capability to store sounds in digital form and then to retrieve those sounds and play them back on demand. The program also allows parcels of sound to be stored as an electronic document. The resulting application deals with the spoken word, not with numbers or the written word, and allows it to be processed in much the same way we have traditionally used computers to process written information.

Sound input and output, especially in the form of speech, will become an increasingly important part of the interaction between the user and the computer. As voice recognition equipment continues to become more powerful and less costly, we will command computers through spoken commands and computers will be able to respond through synthesized voice as well as visual displays.

Evolution of the interaction between the computer and the user will continue. The computer will become steadily easier to use because it will assist the user in choosing the appropriate commands. The computer will be programmed to develop a unique profile for each user based on the user's specified preferences and the recorded history of interaction between the user and the computer. As a result of these innovations, computers will interact with human beings more and more on the terms of human beings and less and less on the terms of computers.

Over the last half of this century, we will have moved from computers that have to be programmed in numbers to computers that are able to converse, albeit in a highly stylized manner, in human language. This transformation in computing technology opens the door to an entirely new view of information and knowledge that has the potential for fundamentally transforming the way in which human beings work, especially human beings in knowledge industries like higher education. Computers are becoming information appliances capable of assisting us in the creation, recording, storage, transmission, and retrieval of information in numeric, written, spoken, pictorial, and algorithmic forms.

Technology, Information, and Human Communication

The need for precise communication is fundamental to modern industrial civilization and to the keeper of its intellectual heritage, the university.

Because the scholarly community is distributed over the earth and across time, the university must have the ability to communicate despite barriers of time and distance. At present, that communication is carried out primarily through the written word on millions and millions of pages of printed and typewritten documents.

Dominance of the written word has resulted mainly from the quality of the technology that supports the production, storage, dissemination, and use of material in written form. Indeed, literacy, that is, the ability to read and write, is universally accepted as a precondition to becoming an educated person.

Historically, communication is one of the first uses found for new technologies. This has been especially true of information technology. Electronics was used early to support the development of mass communication such as radio and television. Electronics was also used to reproduce recordings, first audio recordings and later video recordings. As computers have become steadily more cost-effective and powerful, they have become useful for an increasingly wide variety of communications purposes.

The first use was simply the inputting and editing of text in word processors. This application required relatively little computer power and was first implemented in time-sharing computers. As these facilities became more advanced, they were transformed into full-fledged document production systems that could drive many different types of output devices. Articles could be typeset directly from a computer file.

The first microcomputers also had text-processing capability and as they became more powerful, these tools were also expanded to provide full document production facilities. Today, clusters of microcomputers can share a number of high quality output devices ranging from film recorders to laser printers. As a result, we have a new industry called *desktop publishing* that allows even a small office to produce professional quality documents. Typesetting firms across the nation are more and more prepared to accept manuscripts in electronic form with the result that book publishing is also being done via electronic means. Gutenberg would certainly not recognize the technology used today to produce printed materials.

The Universal Information Appliance

The continued dominance of text in communication among human beings is, however, to a large extent the result of the superior technology that has been developed in support of textual communication. With suitable interfaces, computers can now provide a new medium for human expression, one that is comprehensive across the full range of communication and is sufficiently general purpose to be shared across all disciplines and the arts. The most exciting innovations in communication are likely to come from the increased capabilities of computers to deal with nontextual forms of information.

Modern information technology is rapidly providing a means of dealing just as efficiently and precisely with information in other forms. The increasing capabilities of the paint-and-draw software have provided a substitute for the brush and the pallet in visual expression. High-quality computer graphics packages now enable novices to develop pictorial representations of organizations and processes and to display graphically information formerly conveyed through numeric tables.

The computer's capability to digitize voice and other sounds supports recording and editing audio information. Good voice mail systems duplicate many of the capabilities of the office memorandum and filing systems as well as the advantages of electronic mail for administrative communication. The computer is also being used in the laboratory as the foundation for scientific instrumentation and recording physical phenomena. Increasingly, the computer is playing the roles of a note pad, sketch pad, drafting board, photographic film, and magnetic recorder.

Since computers can be connected to form networks and output devices such as printers and plotters can be attached to them, they can support the transmission and sharing of information. We are beginning to see technology that can generate, store, and transmit a multimedia document, that is, a document that contains written, visual, and audio information. Electronic mail is becoming a substitute for the letter. More and more online services are available that provide the same capabilities now provided by newspapers and magazines. As document delivery and production systems improve, we can expect computer distribution of books, often with selective printing of appropriate sections.

The capability to digitize and store speech allows the computer to provide voice mail service and interact with the telephone system in support of audio communication. The computer is now gaining capability to transmit sound of sufficient quality to satisfy the musician and pictures of adequate quality to satisfy the artist. As a result, computers will be integrated with radio and television to play an important role in mass communications.

In summary, the capability of information technology to provide a comprehensive technology for the creation, recording, and storage as well as subsequent transmission and sharing of information in all forms from all disciplines provides an opportunity for a new flowering of interdisciplinary communication. The result is likely to be a radical transformation of scholarly communication. The ability to communicate in all of these forms and to appropriately interweave these forms of communication will soon be as important to effective scholarly intercourse as is the ability to manipulate information in written form today.

Algorithmic Information

While the convergence of written, visual, and audio information into the document of the future is important and will undoubtedly create major changes in higher education, the impact of a new form of information that has resulted from the advent of the stored program computer is likely to have an even more significant impact. This information might best be called "algorithmic information" because it is expressed in an algorithm or a computer program.

Algorithmic information is fundamentally different from other forms of information because algorithmic information is effective even when it is not understood by its user. Prior to the application of algorithmic information to statistics, for example, if a scholar wished to undertake a factor analysis, she was required to study a statistics text that described the way in which matrices of relationships could be further analyzed to discern underlying factors. In so doing, she had to learn about such topics of matrix algebra as eigenvalues and determinants. Only after learning at least the rudiments of these mathematical manipulations would she be able to process data in such a way as to create a factor analysis.

Starting in the 1960s, statisticians, numerical analysts, and computer programmers created computer programs that read information from punched cards and manipulated that information so as to perform a factor analysis and output the results on a printer. Suddenly, social scientists no longer needed to understand the mathematics of factor analysis. All that was necessary was arranging information on punched cards for appropriate computer interpretation and enough knowledge about the results of factor analysis to appropriately interpret the computer output. In other words, the scholar no longer had to understand factor analysis to do factor analysis.

Algorithmic information has now penetrated every corner of life. Bell Laboratories has produced a computer program that analyzes written text to spot poor usage of the English language. Microwave ovens that are programmed to roast meat appropriately are being built. Automobiles now contain computers that not only coordinate the functioning of the engine but its interaction with the transmission, the fuel system, the driver, and the road. Engineers use computer programs to assist in the design of circuits and to analyze the way in which those circuits function before they are even built. Algorithmic information is now found and being used broadly throughout our civilization.

Algorithmic information's very nature guarantees its impact on higher education. An algorithm not only transmits information in a precise form across time and distance, but also enables action to be taken at a place and at a time remote from the person who originally formulated the plan for that action.

As a result, algorithmic information may generate consequences unintended by its creator. All of us in the social sciences have encountered articles in which algorithmic information was inappropriately used in the processing of data and mistaken conclusions resulted. This inappropriate use was not a result of any fraudulent tendency on the part of the researcher, but rather because the researcher used an algorithm that was not appropriate for the particular problem being investigated.

This highlights the fact that algorithmic information does not include an important element of quality control which is included in the acquisition and use of most other forms of information. If a scholar decides to use information that is described in written form to carry out a procedure, first of all he must read that description and understand it. As a result, he can make his own check for logical consistency. Assuming prior knowledge of the field, he can check for consistency with other knowledge. In most cases, however, when algorithmic information is used, the scholar does not analyze the structure of the computer program. In many cases, such analysis is forbidden because the computer program is a trade secret and not available for examination. As a result, the scholar is totally dependent on the quality of the algorithm's originator and implementers for correct functioning of the algorithm.

Despite the potential for misuse and dangers inherent in algorithmic information, it is one of the most powerful forms of information we have. Because algorithmic information does not demand user knowledge for successful use, it has a unique potential for rapidly multiplying human capability and has profound implications for education.

I will not soon forget a heated discussion between two professors of electrical engineering, both of whom were highly respected for their attention to teaching and the promising character of their research. One of those professors proposed that much of the time spent teaching electrical engineers to do elementary circuit analysis was no longer a necessary part of the electrical engineering curriculum because high quality algorithmic knowledge that allowed students to design and simulate the operation of basic electronic circuit elements was available. The other professor was absolutely aghast that his colleague would have the audacity to suggest that an electrical engineer graduate without having developed and extensively practiced elementary electronic analysis. To him, that knowledge was fundamental to all understanding of electrical engineering.

The first professor argued that the time saved in not teaching such basic circuit analysis could be better used in helping engineers analyze systems of electronic circuits and advanced configurations of those systems. He argued with some intensity that graduate engineers had far too little experience and knowledge about such complex electronic systems and were, therefore, ill prepared when they began their practice as professional engineers.

While this argument had some of the elements of a religious discussion, it was probably not too different from arguments that must have occurred among scholars regarding the necessity of understanding Latin and Greek as a foundation for a high quality liberal education. In fact, we in higher education are constantly engaged in trading off the need for broad, general, and foundation knowledge with the need for deep detailed understanding of the more advanced aspects of our professions and specialties. Algorithmic information provides us with yet another means by which we can more effectively allocate the use of our students' time.

Like all of the trade-offs that we have undertaken in the past, this is a trade-off that must not be considered lightly. If we can, however, develop appropriate means of allowing our students to stand on the shoulders of their predecessors by using the algorithms of their predecessors, we may be able to advance education in some very fundamental ways. At a minimum, providing students with exposure to the algorithms developed by their intellectual forbearers may be a highly effective way of educating them about the knowledge generated by their predecessors.

The University Library and Scholarly Publication

The Heritage of the Library

The university library has been, since the beginning, the dominant centrally provided service to support scholarship at the great universities of the world. Not surprisingly, institutions dedicated to the creation and transmission of knowledge create and maintain, often as a central symbol of those efforts, a large organization that preserves and provides access to knowledge produced over the past centuries. From the point of view of a scholar, whether that scholar be a researcher, creative artist, or student, the library stands for easy access to enormous amounts of information.

The modern research library is remarkable, not only for volume of information storage, but for quality of information retrieval provided. Nowhere else in our society does there exist an organization that will usually, in an hour's time, help a patron find most of the fundamental as well as recent developments in almost any field of human knowledge. The libraries have developed an intricate, highly specialized structure mainly supported by the human skills of librarians to make this access possible.

The Challenge to the Library

At the same time, academic libraries today are sorely challenged. The cost of acquiring the basic materials, the books and journals that form the foundation of the libraries' ability to serve its clients, is steadily increasing. Many of the materials already acquired are in a state of decay and massive efforts will be required to preserve them for future scholars. New forms of information and new patterns of information use generated by the steady advance of information technology not only provide the libraries with an opportunity to improve the services they offer, but also challenge them to expand into new areas precisely when they are having trouble maintaining their traditional strengths.

Library staff salaries are not usually competitive with the salaries offered by the information technology industry. Even schools of library science, which have in the past provided the foundation staff for academic libraries, find more and more of their graduates going off into other areas of the information industry and not into the library.

In summary, there are enormous demands on the university library to simply maintain the quality of its traditional services. But, at the same time, the library is being asked to move into new areas and use new technologies to deliver its services. In many libraries, this set of imperatives is creating important tensions about the fundamental values of librarianship.

One of the most important roles of the library is to preserve information and lead the scholar to comprehensive information on a particular subject. This has led, reasonably enough, to a set of conservative practices that range all the way from materials acquisition through cataloging and reference services. For instance, duplication in acquisitions, even among cooperating libraries, is done not only to support easy local access for scholars, but also to guarantee that if an item is lost or damaged, it will be available from another library for subsequent use.

The objective of comprehensive access means that the library catalog needs to include all holdings to ensure that scholars will find all relevant information on a particular subject. Conversion to an automated online catalog is therefore complicated by concern that scholars will use only the records in a temporarily incomplete electronic catalog and fail to plumb the full resources of the library.

Since libraries play such an important part in the preservation of information and because scholars have learned to depend on libraries for comprehensive access to information, it can be argued that the information technology culture of the library should be conservative and should undertake change only after careful consideration and strong consensus on the part of the library community. That desirable conservative approach is being challenged by an increasing demand for change stemming from advances in information technology and economic forces. All of these forces, however, are combining to change the approach of libraries to their activities.

Changes in the publishing industry will change the way in which libraries acquire material. Changes in storage technology will challenge the dominance of the book and journal for information storage. High quality, integrated systems will change not only the operation of the library, but more importantly, the way in which its patrons gain access to the library's material. New printing and reproduction technologies will change the manner in which the library delivers its material. The ability to deal with new forms of information, especially algorithmic information, will require the library to adapt its capabilities to provide patron access to the new forms of information.

The Publication Process and Acquisitions

Libraries are challenged by the cost of acquiring materials and scholars are handicapped by the long delay between the development of new knowledge and its eventual appearance on the library shelf. An electronically facilitated publishing environment could have a positive impact on both the cost and the currency of information in the libraries.

Scholars in almost all fields develop and share information in a remarkably similar fashion. A faculty member typically starts a publication by developing an outline of the area she wishes to cover. She might well share the outline with a small group of colleagues, perhaps using a national network. The scholar then produces a rough draft of the paper and, at some point, shares that draft with a few close associates and colleagues. At that stage, the paper is typically a typescript and has been reproduced via photocopier. The paper is quite often already in digital form in a word processor. In some fields, the draft is likely to have already been shared with other scholars over communication networks.

After gaining feedback from colleagues, the scholar will typically present a version of the paper at a scholarly conference and distribute copies of the paper at that conference, but not for attribution. In some cases, the paper will actually be incorporated into a set of conference proceedings and be published for the first time. After feedback, the scholar is likely to refine and enhance the paper and submit it to a professional journal in her field for peer review and publication. Usually, by this time, the paper has been read and the material is familiar to as many as a hundred other scholars working in closely related areas.

Only with its publication in proceedings or journal does the paper enter a public bibliography and become available to students and scholars throughout the world. The delay from the initial creation of the paper to its broad availability is partly due to its iterative refinement. Scholars do not wish to provide their papers for broad distribution until they are confident that they have thought through all of the issues in a careful fashion.

There are, however, other delays in the process, often as long as a year or more, that are simply a result of time constants built into the review and journal publication process. The library acquisition and cataloging process can often add additional delays, especially to information that ultimately finds its way into book form rather than into a scholarly journal.

Unfortunately, libraries are increasingly pressed for the budgetary support required to provide a comprehensive set of periodical subscriptions and to purchase the full set of scholarly monographs published in all of the fields covered by the modern university. As a result, the process of scholarly publication and distribution becomes steadily more expensive, continues to be slow, and declines in the quality of its coverage due to budgetary pressures.

Publishers are powerless to interrupt this trend for, as the cost continues to increase, rising prices require that publication costs must be recovered with steadily smaller publication runs. The specialization of certain publishers in scholarly materials means that there is less and less opportunity for substantial cross-subsidization of scholarly publications by more popular and profitable publications. Furthermore, while the process could be organized differently and thereby substantially reduce costs, publishers are prevented by antitrust rulings from collaborating to achieve those new approaches.

Universities, working through their libraries, information technology organizations and, where available, university presses, are likely to be able to provide a new direction for scholarly publication. Many university scholars already produce the early drafts of their publications on personal computers. More are using personal computers all the time, if not directly, then through secretarial support. Those microcomputers are increasingly tied together through university networks that allow for the transmission of papers within the university and their subsequent sharing among scholars.

Most of the research universities in the United States and an increasingly large proportion of all institutions of higher education are being networked together so that information can be moved from the campus network of one university to that of another. We are also beginning to see the emergence of standards for the production of publication quality information, not only printed text, but also pictorial and graphic information. Modern laser printer technology allows on-demand printing with quite acceptable quality. In other words, the technological structure for electronic publication is already in place in many universities and will shortly be in place in almost all institutions of higher education.

Some modest organizational changes and investments would produce an environment in which individual scholars could use these capabilities to write and publish their scholarly work and acquire the scholarly work of others. Electronic publication mechanisms could be created which would interact directly with the scholar and depend on the library for direct "publication."

For example, when the scholar had refined her paper to the point that she wished to make it available to other scholars that she did not know, the library could catalog the unpublished paper so it could be found and read by scholars throughout the community. To avoid overburdening the cataloging staff, the scholar herself would interact with an expert system that would guide her through the development of a preliminary cataloging record that would be inserted in the library's online catalog with a special notation indicating it was a preliminary catalog record.

When the scholar decided that she wished to submit the article to a journal, she would send an electronic mail message to the editor of the journal suggesting that the journal's panel of reviewers critique the article. She would, of course, send along an electronic copy of the article. The review panel might suggest further changes in the article but, assuming that it was finally accepted for publication, the article would simply be included in the table of contents of that electronic journal.

The library would be notified electronically that an addition had been made to the table of contents. At that point, the informal catalog record would be reviewed by the journal and by the cataloging staff preparatory to inclusion in the library's online catalog. The paper would then gain the status of full publication. A similar process would occur in the case of a book publication, but with a publisher (perhaps a university press) replacing the journal review board.

Libraries would install facilities that provide for the printing on demand of electronic publications. Scholars, through their professional societies, would organize review panels that decide whether a particular paper already in electronic form meets the standards of quality required for inclusion in the table of contents of an electronic publication. University presses would distribute electronic versions of books for on-demand printing.

The library would not only avoid many of the costs involved in subscribing to a printed journal or buying a book but would also become a more integral part of the active scholarly life of the university by capturing publications for broad access at an early stage in their creation.

Higher education, working cooperatively, could create a new model for the publication of scholarly information that would substantially reduce the time lags currently experienced, reduce the costs and thereby increase the coverage and comprehensiveness of accessible information, and encourage more cross-disciplinary communication.

Storage

Digitization, storage densities, and low cost of the new optical and magneto-optical disc technologies will allow consideration of the storage of all types of publications. Compact audio discs are the first of the mass produced items published in this fashion but as the compact disc is used increasingly to provide access to graphical, pictorial and algorithmic information, publication in digital form will expand substantially. As relatively inexpensive record and playback optical discs become available, far more information will be stored much more compactly. Preservation of materials will also become a less critical problem.

Information Retrieval

Many libraries have now begun to provide their patrons with access to an online catalog that provides the ability to access and find information more conveniently and effectively than the card catalog has provided in the past. While important tensions exist during the periods of retrospective conversion of the card catalog to the new electronic form, especially for the large research library, the online catalog provides scholars with easy access to the library's bibliographic resources from the faculty office or the student desk. That information can be used to help build a local bibliography in support of the scholar's active work as well as obtain information about publications of interest.

There is an important set of new challenges in the bibliographic area, however, relating to the cataloging of new forms of information. As computers become more widespread across university campuses and facilitate production of larger quantities of information in audio, visual and algorithmic form, there will be an increasing amount of information output in these new forms. While the library community has developed a superb set of tools for access to information in written form, development is still needed on tools and procedures for access to information in these other forms.

The need is already enormous and growing rapidly. In the area of algorithmic information alone, the number of new computer programs that are useful for scholarly purposes is growing at an exponential rate. These programs come from a variety of sources, some commercial, some not-for-profit, and some private. People are reinventing algorithms to perform similar tasks almost every hour across this nation today. Because there is no comprehensive source of information about existing algorithms, there is no organization on most university campuses into which a faculty member or student can enter a request for information concerning a particular type of algorithm. Even if such a service exists, it does not provide the same type of assistance and comprehensive access to information which would be available in response to a request for written information in the university library.

Only the library community has the systems and the skills necessary to comprehend such a vast and rapidly growing array of information. The information technology industry has not yet recognized its need to be tied to the library community. This is an area of important future service for libraries and represents a significant challenge to their well-formulated and finely honed approaches to making information available to a broad spectrum of patrons.

Delivery

Changes in storage and information retrieval might happen without a substantial change in library information delivery mechanisms, but that would be highly unlikely. Libraries increasingly deliver information to patrons who then photocopy a small section of that information for inclusion in their permanent files. By the same token, as an increasing amount of information becomes available through the electronic networks, users will want to extract segments of that information for use in their scholarship and hold those segments of information in their local information environment. Furthermore, users will print document segments using the increasingly cost-effective capabilities of laser printers.

As a result, more and more delivery of materials will be done in electronic form. At the same time, the ability of a scholar to determine that a particular item is available in the library through the online cataloging system will result in a demand for an online circulation system through which that same user can enter a request for the material to be delivered for further study even when the material is not in electronic form.

The results will be a much higher level of overall patronage and demand on library materials and of use of more library materials outside the confines of the library itself. These changes will affect the life of the materials, the ease with which the materials can be found in the library, and change the economics of serving the user population.

All of these trends ignore the increasing ability of electronic catalogs to facilitate interlibrary loan through which the resources of the great research libraries can be made available across a much broader spectrum of the population and over broader geographic areas. For physical materials, as opposed to electronic materials, the library will be increasingly challenged with a set of policy considerations regarding the extent to which it should circulate materials beyond the local environment with the consequent chance that a local scholar will find the material unavailable.

In summary, then, as libraries become part of the overall information technology environment on many of our campuses, there will be fundamental changes in the way they serve their clients, in the way they acquire and preserve information, and in the types of materials upon which they concentrate their efforts. While these changes will undoubtedly lead to improvements in information access in a number of ways, they could, if mismanaged, damage some of the values that scholars have come to depend on libraries to provide.

Systems Architecture
for Higher Education

In view of the changing role of information technology and changes in the technology itself, the type of information technology systems architecture that is most suitable for applications in higher education has changed dramatically over the last twenty years. In the late 50s and early 60s, computers were used primarily for computational tasks by a minority of the university community, mostly scientists and statisticians. People went to the computer center and submitted decks of punched cards that were batched into a continuous stream of jobs to be processed by the computer. Since the focus of that activity was on the computer itself and since there were major scale economies in the acquisition of computers, the computing center concept rapidly evolved as the use of computers spread beyond the initial users and became a resource for the full university.

With the advent of time-sharing or interactive computing, the focus began to shift away from the computing center itself as telecommunications provided remote access to the computer. People no longer went to the computing center to do their computing but worked from laboratories or offices spread across the university. The focus of the processing and information storage, however, was still in the central computer because of the continuing scale economies. During this period, the use of computers also broadened to include activities in the humanities and information retrieval as well as the traditional efforts in the sciences, mathematics, and statistics.

During this same period of batch and interactive computing, many universities started to develop facilities to carry out administrative tasks by a computer, copying corporate information system environments to perform functions like payroll and accounting. In most universities separate organizations were established to carry out the administrative functions. This was partly because such functions were carried out through a different portion of the universities' organizational structure and partly because the software tools and the computers that supported academic and research activities were not well suited to supporting administrative functions.

As computers became steadily more cost-effective, the range of users on both the academic and administrative sides steadily broadened. The number of users with convenient access to computer terminals became a significant portion of the overall community in many universities. In the universities with the most aggressive programs, the overall budget for computing activities began to approach 5 percent of the institutional budget and increasing attention was paid to the management and strategic importance of computing in the university.

The advent in the early 1970s of the minicomputer caused a discontinuity in the historical pattern of scale economies that resulted from the acquisition of large computers. A laboratory suddenly could obtain computing power less expensively through a locally owned machine than through a centrally purchased machine. This trend was reinforced by decisions made in the national science funding agencies, particularly the National Science Foundation, to withdraw support from the central campus computing centers and to fund researchers to purchase their own laboratory computing facilities.

The rapid expansion of laboratory minicomputers moved the focus of the information technology environment farther away from the central computing facility than had the earlier advent of networks to support time-sharing. In only a few universities was any systematic effort made to connect the laboratory minicomputer to the universities' central computing facility. Universities that had provided conservative funding levels to the central computing facility found the minicomputer trend especially strong because the central facility was not able to effectively compete with the laboratory facilities. Thus began a phenomenon that has become known as the VAXcination[7] of university computing. Many computing centers fell on hard times and suffered substantial reductions in quality of service and staff while the decentralized facilities became most important from the user point of view.

In the late 1970s the microcomputer started to have impact on the university information technology environment. Especially as high-quality word processing software became available on these machines, faculty and students purchased it by the tens of thousands. In universities with high-quality, central interactive computing services and good net-works, these microcomputers were often connected to the networks as a simulated computer terminal. In most universities, however, the microcomputers were not network-connected. The microcomputer decentralized the information technology environment more rapidly than ever before.

A systems architecture strategy for higher education must be built on the enormous benefits of microcomputers and departmental minicom-puters. Not only do the new types of computer provide access to substan-tial computing at low cost, but they also stimulate distributed investment. Given the pressure on university financial resources, that coinvestment has become critical to expanding student and faculty access to informa-tion technology.

At the same time, the radical decentralization of computing in the university has created substantial liabilities. Information sharing among users has become more difficult because information is often contained in a hardware and software environment not compatible with another user's environment. Thus, while either an Apple Macintosh or an IBM personal computer can be used to produce a high-quality document, that document cannot be transferred from the Apple to the IBM without substantial effort. The problem is not simply one of network connec-tions or even compatibility of disc storage, but extends further to the operating systems and applications software available on both systems.

Even applications produced by the same software manufacturer often do not provide for easy exchange of information. For instance, a document produced using Microsoft Word on the IBM personal com-puter until recently could not be transferred with full formatting to the Apple Macintosh also using Microsoft Word. The microcomputer has the potential increasingly to isolate scholars from one another. This isola-tion has important negative implications for the way in which colleagues will share information and the way in which students will interact and work together with each other and faculty.

The lack of good network connections has meant that users are increasingly limited to carrying out only those tasks that can be effec-tively accomplished with their local computing environment. For instance, the production of really high quality printed output is difficult when the only printer attached to your personal computer is a dot matrix printer. Also, the accomplishment of really large-scale computational tasks is difficult if your personal computer and your departmental minicomputer are not linked to a large-scale computing resource. Indeed, the lack of access to supercomputers is now often cited as one of the unfortunate consequences of the increasing decentralization of university computing environments. The result is that a number of science applications have not been attempted simply because large-scale computing resources were not conveniently available.

In summary, the systems architecture for higher education must take into account these past trends, the economic realities, and the need that the university especially has to share information and resources. All of these considerations lead to an information technology environment for the future of higher education centered on an institutionwide information network, based on broad access to personal workstations, enhanced by a diverse set of serveral facilities, and integrated through a coherent software environment. These four elements will together provide the highest function, lowest cost growth path in the use of information technology for higher education.

Institutionwide Information Network

Distribution of processing power across a geographically decentralized range of equipment has substantial advantages but also has a major potential liability. An information utility should support users in their private efforts and provide a facility for collaboration among users. Time-sharing systems not only allowed users to share processing capabilities but also facilitated information storage and exchange. Services ranging from library access to electronic mail are critically dependent on a central information storage and retrieval facility. The need for these capabilities in the coming era will be fulfilled through an institutionwide information network. If appropriately designed and implemented, that network will become the fundamental central facility for future information storage and processing environments. The characteristics of such a network are sketched out below.

Information Storage as well as Information Transport

The capabilities of the network are especially important to higher education. Colleges and universities give high priority to facilitating inquisitive behavior. The fundamental rule of university life is that information should be broadly accessible, not restricted to those who have the need to know. Any information storage and retrieval system that compartmentalizes users one from another is undesirable. Therefore, the network should not only provide communications to other workstations and facilities, but should also be the default repository for information developed on a workstation.

The current focus of network developers and implementers is transporting information from one computational node to another. Obviously, the capability to explicitly move information across the network is a fundamental requirement and allows sharing of information among coworkers. The file system of a time-sharing system, however, implements a broader capability. All users of the system can access stored information from wherever they are using the system. The system further provides facilities that allow multiuser access to be controlled. Access to the latest version of the information is thereby ensured and updates from multiple sources can be coordinated. Most networks of personal computers provide significantly less broad access to and control of information because the primary file system is assumed to be in each user's workstation rather than being a shared central capability. The network required by higher education should provide information storage as well as information transport.

Multimedia Capability

The future university will depend on its ability to utilize algorithmic, audio, and video information just as it now depends on its ability to use written information. As technology advances, computer algorithms, the spoken word, graphs and pictures will increasingly be integrated into documents along with written material. The network must have the capability and capacity to effectively store, transmit, and retrieve information of all types. The market is just now beginning to provide systems that integrate text, voice, and graphical information. Network planning for digitized voice and video should therefore be coordinated with planning for data.

Ubiquity

The information network must be everywhere. A network that provides access only to a segment of the community excludes others from full participation in the environment. In a university or college, such access can only be provided by a plan that includes faculty and staff offices, student and faculty residences, laboratories and classrooms. An information appliance should be as easily plugged in as a typewriter but in a wider variety of locations. For instance, outlets would be useful in library study areas and at every seat of selected classrooms and laboratories.

Geographic Coverage

A larger and larger proportion of professional work time is being spent outside the office in the home environment. Work away from the office has always been a dominant feature of the university environment. Most faculty have studies at home and students have no offices at all. As a result, the network capabilities must extend beyond the physical boundaries of the campus. This need represents one of the largest potential growth areas for telephone operating companies and is sure to be rapidly developed and broadly exploited.

Sabbatical periods and scholarly travel have already created a demand for even broader geographic coverage. As students who have become accustomed to the capabilities of a network-centered information technology environment graduate, they will want continued access after they leave the campus. Universities and colleges will use the technology to provide graduates with continuing education. Increasingly, courses that use information technology as a delivery mechanism will be taught to students beyond the geographic confines of the campus. As a result, the network plan should include the capability to support worldwide access.

Inter-institutional Connectivity

In our increasingly interdependent information society, a network that simply provides high-quality information transport and storage within a single institution is not adequate. An increasingly large amount of the information needed by any university is externally generated and is available through a multiplicity of external networks. Those networks range from the restricted special-purpose networks such as ARPANET and CSNET to higher education networks such as BITNET and MAILNET. There are a number of common carrier networks such as TYMNET, Telenet, and Autonet. Using these common carrier networks are a variety of information services and other logical networks such as The Source, MCI mail, and Dow Jones. Local networks must provide high-quality interfaces to these external networks.

Adaptability and Expansibility

Technology will continue to change and cause associated change in workstations, servers, and the network itself. Colleges and universities already have a substantial installed base of equipment. They must be able to adapt the existing technology to the networked environment. Most institutions begin installation of the network-based system with a modest initial effort but expect to expand the coverage of the system by several orders of magnitude over its life. Many users in the higher education environment view use of the newest technology as an end in itself. As a result, the network must be designed with the capability to adapt to new technology and to be expanded without disruption to the community.

Standards

The most effective means of meeting the requirements for adaptability and expansibility is to base the network design on national and international standards. The diversity of workstations typical of the higher education environment requires that the network not constrain the choice of attached nodes even though the network itself must be of homogeneous design to provide an integrated central communications information utility. The network architecture must present a well-defined, flexible interface to the workstation and server software. A variety of different software architectures can then be designed to interact with that interface.

Security

The use of a network for information storage in addition to transmission makes network security even more important. If users are not convinced of that security, they will refuse to store information in the network. On the other hand, if the security provisions are inconvenient or add significantly to cost, the network will fall into disuse and information will be stored in less secure distributed facilities.

Reliability

As the information technology environment becomes fundamental to instruction, it needs to become as reliable as the blackboard and the telephone. Faculty and students will not trust their important work to an unreliable network. In fact, reliability is probably the most important design goal of the overall network environment. That reliability must include both dependable access to the network and integrity of the information stored in the network.

Distributed Control

Many universities will have networks with literally tens of thousands of attached workstation and servers. The network must not become a bottleneck to the exchange of information. No foreseeable central computer can provide communications and information sharing for so large a network. As a result, the network will have to support a number of cooperating servers of modest size rather than large unitary servers. The design should place the largest possible proportion of demand for computation on the attached nodes and not depend on a central node to mediate communications except where absolutely necessary. The information network must therefore provide communication on a peer to peer basis as well as on a hierarchical basis.

Local Area Subnetworks

No networking solution will meet all needs for a complex multiobjective organization such as a major university. Local subnetworks will continue to be an important part of the overall information technology environment and these local subnetworks must be easily accommodated and connected with the institutional network. As a result, there must be a continuing investment in interface and gateway technology between the local subnetworks and the institutional networks.

Network Services

To support information storage as well as information transmission, the network must support three related services. First, the network must be able to find by name, any object stored in it, on demand, from any attached computational node. Second, the network must be able to determine whether the user or other active agent seeking access to information is authorized to have such access. The network, therefore, must incorporate a name server and an authorization server to facilitate control-access to stored information.

Third, as an increasingly large number of services are provided by the network, there is increasing potential value in having the network offer access-control and accounting services to the attached systems. Lodging such capabilities in the network facilitates the addition of new services to the network and ensures integration of network administration with the operation of the overall environment.

Conclusion

The institutional information network will be the focal point of tomorrow's higher education computing environment. The network will not only provide communication services among thousands of workstations, servers, and other networks, but will provide the central information resource for the institution. The network will enable knowledge-sharing among students and faculty; unify disciplines across institutional boundaries; support the integration of written, voice, graphical, pictorial, and algorithmic information; facilitate interactions between personal workstations and specialized server facilities; and provide the foundation for software coherence across the institution. In other words, the information network will occupy the institutional niche formally occupied by the central computer.

Workstation-based Computing

The most visible manifestation of microelectronics has been the broad proliferation of personal computers throughout our society. The personal computer workstation's role in the information technology architecture is crucial.

Cost Effectiveness

The low cost and convenience of the personal computer or "information appliance" has led to a mass market that has resulted in comparatively low prices. Computational capacity in personal computers is now much less expensive than equivalent mainframe capacity. Furthermore, the attractiveness of personal workstations has led to substantial breadth of funding for their acquisition. Since the workstations are viewed by the users as their personal information appliance, universities have succeeded in creating a mixed investment strategy where the user provides a proportion of the funds for the acquisition of the workstation and the organization provides the remainder. Numerous manufacturers have been willing to provide substantial discounts and grants of equipment to higher education that further reduce the cost and spread the base of investment. As a result, the level of investment in computational capacity is no longer constrained entirely by central organizational budgets but now comes from a variety of sources.

User Interface Quality

Modern personal workstations provide far more effective interaction with the user. Computational power is located close to the devices through which the user communicates, whether that device be a keyboard, a graphic screen, a microphone, or a speaker. The interactions between the computer and the user are therefore unconstrained by the cost of connecting user interface devices with the computer. As a consequence, the computer and its user are able to use graphics and sound as well as keyboarded and displayed characters to enhance communications.

The fact that the computer is dedicated to the use of a single person has a profound effect on the designer's view of feasible applications. In a time-sharing system, an important economic constraint was that the system had to serve a large number of users without noticeably delaying any one user's request. The system therefore had to be economical in computing power per user. In fact, one of the measures of effectiveness often used to describe a time-sharing system was the number of simultaneous users it could successfully support.

The result was that programs requiring substantial computation to support user interaction were not successful in the time-sharing environment. Time-sharing users have been encouraged to specify exactly what they wish the computer to do, usually in a way that is narrowly constrained and substantially less flexible than the average human interaction.

A personal computer, on the other hand, provides substantially more computational capability that is dedicated to a single user. Much more easily used and comfortable styles of interaction between the user and a personal computer are possible. Pioneering work was done in this area at Xerox's Palo Alto Research Center and has been adopted and deployed widely on personal computers made by other manufacturers. The result is that using a computer is much less work and feels substantially more natural. Taken to its current extreme, the so-called video game is the best example of how enjoyable interaction with a personal computer can be made.

Availability of Applications

The quality of the user interface and the relatively low cost offered by personal workstations have translated into a strong market for innovative applications software. The most creative computing applications are now being developed for personal workstations. The applications that have enhanced the productivity of information workers most significantly over the last five years have been developed for personal workstations.

The spreadsheet application is the best example. The electronic spreadsheet is now viewed as a standard, almost obligatory tool for the full spectrum of management activities. The success of the spreadsheet depends critically on the personal workstation's close coupling to its display and the dedicated computing power available to the user. The result is a major improvement in the capability of managers to investigate alternatives and develop an intuitive grasp of the interrelations important to effective management.

Ubiquity of Access

The outcome, then, is that an increasingly large proportion of knowledge workers are using personal computers routinely to accomplish their objectives. The majority of that activity is not focused so much on the computational capacity of their workstations, but rather on their capability to process information. A number of universities have already reached the state where virtually every faculty member and student has a personal workstation and many have more than one. Such broad access to this new generation of information appliances is a necessary, but not sufficient, condition for a high quality information technology environment. As outlined, those machines need to be interconnected with the network and connected via a network to a set of other specialized and powerful facilities called servers.

Server Facilities

While most of the computation done in the computing environment of the 1990s will be carried out in workstations and most of the information will be stored in the network, inevitably there will be types of computation that the workstations will be unable to perform and types of information that will not be well suited to management in this network file system. Furthermore, the computing environment must be strongly connected to the external world through provision of means of input and output of information and control of other related systems such as design and manufacturing facilities. As a result, the information environment will include substantial server facilities.

Computation Servers

The easiest servers to predict are the various types of computation servers. As computing technology continues to advance, an increasingly wide variety of computational engines is becoming available. There are vector-oriented supercomputers, massive parallel supercomputers, systems designed primarily to execute production systems for artificial intelligence research, and other special purpose computational facilities such as image processors and signal processors. The network should allow any workstation to use any appropriate computation server whether that computation server is directly attached to the local network or, as is likely for expensive servers, attached via some external network.

Information Servers

Simply providing an institutionwide file system does not answer the needs of the users for access to information. In particular, database servers and index servers are probably also necessary. *Database servers* would provide specialized access to information not easily organized in the architecture in the shared filing system. Thus, for instance, a database server might provide access to personnel records, student transcripts, or accounting information. In many cases, such database servers will provide the path for transition from large central administrative applications to more distributed implementations of those same applications where the user interface is managed locally but access to the complex data structure is provided through the central database server. In other cases, information would appropriately reside in the file system, but access to that information will require a more complex index structure than the file system itself provides. To meet this need, index servers could be added to the network for access to information contained in the file system. *Index servers,* for instance, might be appropriate to provide access and easy retrieval of documents stored within the file system. As other information environments become increasingly integrated with the library information environment, index servers of this type will become increasingly important. I envision a future where most publication is done through the transmission of electronic text to an index server that provides the physical embodiment of today's card catalog or professional journal. That text then would be available on demand to users of the network.

Finally, current time-sharing systems are proving to be powerful vehicles for interpersonal communication in the form of electronic mail, electronic conferencing, and electronic bulletin boards. While all of these systems can be built on top of the file system in the information network, *special application servers* may be necessary to appropriately index and maintain these services for large organizations.

While at one time the view of the future information environment was the view of the "paperless" office, we have learned that the ability to move information electronically onto permanent hard copy has simply been reinforced by the capabilities of our electronic information environments. In particular, the network must allow access to print servers that provide output ranging from rough drafts of documents to typeset-quality documents ready for publication, to graphic servers that can output graphics and image information to paper and microforms and machine-readable output for transport to otherwise unconnected information networks.

Since a substantial number of potentially valuable information sources will not be connected to any electronic network, the network must provide for input of additional information. The network needs the capability to add machinery to pull information coming from any number of different media, ranging from magnetic type to digital laser discs. Furthermore, information in the form of text, image, or audio can be digitized for input to the network. Servers ranging from page readers to interfaces to the institutional telephone system must be provided to allow input of such information.

Implementation and Production Servers

An increasingly large portion of the activity toward which the network is oriented is the actual physical implementation or production of an artifact or process. Thus, for instance, the user doing computer-aided design of an integrated circuit ultimately needs to have that circuit actually produced for testing and subsequent introduction into other equipment. In fact, advanced students at a number of universities can now develop such circuit designs and use the network to have those circuits actually produced by a silicon foundry. As we continue to make progress in computer-aided design and manufacturing, we should expect an increasingly broad need for the attachment of such implementation and production servers to our networks so that designs can be directly rendered into final products, whether those products be motion pictures or machine tools.

Integrated Software Environment

While a computing system consisting of powerful workstations and information network and server facilities can deliver high-quality information processing, its full potential will not be realized without integrating software.

Achieving software integration throughout such a system, however, is a more difficult goal than designing and deploying the other elements of the system. The variety of workstation software environments, many of which support valuable existing applications, is substantial. At this time there is little integration with software to support servers and to deliver information from the network automatically to the workstation. Nonetheless, the value of an integrated software environment is high enough to warrant its coverage of a substantial portion of the system. Such an environment should provide automatic access from the workstation to the information network and servers. There should be a small number of common user interfaces across most of the workstations available in the system. The software should probably be based on an interprocess communication strategy among the workstations, network, and servers. Finally, the software must be compatible with workstations already available as well as new workstations that will have a broad range of capabilities.

Standard User Interfaces

Perhaps the most important characteristic of the integrated software environment will be that the user must learn only a few standard user interfaces to access the full capabilities of the system. At the present time, the two most popular user interfaces are the ones developed by Microsoft and used on the IBM and IBM-compatible workstations and developed by Apple for its Macintosh computers. A less powerful interface, but one that is widely used for developmental purposes, is the UNIX interface that actually exists in a variety of forms. We will see continued development of window-based user interfaces such as those developed for the Macintosh, but with more flexibility and capabilities for multitasking. These new interfaces will probably run on top of a UNIX environment thereby shielding the user from the somewhat arcane user interfaces that are part of the standard UNIX operating systems. Furthermore, they will have the capability to run guest user interfaces such as the Apple Macintosh and IBM/MS-DOS interfaces. Work to support this type of interoperation of a variety of user interfaces is already underway at a number of sites across the United States. As a result, while special needs and a continuing desire for experimentation will continue to contribute variety to user interfaces, it is reasonable to expect that an institution could standardize on one UNIX-based user interface that provides support for several other standard user interfaces and thereby unifies the way in which the computer interacts with its user.

Automatic Access to System Resources

While a common user interface on the workstation provides a partial solution to ease of use, automatic access to the system's other resources is also required. In particular, the user should not have to learn an additional set of conventions to secure information from the network file system or to use most of the servers attached to the network.

Those resources should appear to be part of the workstation environment. Thus, for instance, when the user wishes to access a file, the file should appear to reside in the local workstation and access should be obtained simply by naming the appropriate object. By the same token, when a computational task outstrips the capability of the workstation and requires the resources of one of the computer servers attached to the network, access to that computer server should be automatic and perhaps take place without the knowledge of the user. In other words, access to system resources outside the workstation should be mediated by software in the workstation itself. I believe that the access will be based on a set of interprocess communication conventions that will allow processes in the workstation to interact with those in the file system and network servers. Thus, when the user asks for printed output of a particular document, the workstation will initiate two cooperating processes; one in the file system, and another on a print server to transform the document from its digital image to a paper copy. All the user needs to do is request the printed output. To give another example, a user who requests that a chip be fabricated based on a design developed using the workstation's design capabilities will initiate a process that transfers that design from the file system to a microelectronic fabrication facility for production.

No integrated software environment is likely to be accepted unless it also provides an improved level of service for existing hardware and software. While automatic access to system facilities may not be possible from existing workstations and servers, explicit transfer of files and simulated terminal access should provide expanded capabilities. For instance, a user with an Apple Macintosh should be able to transfer a file from the network to the Macintosh for processing and subsequent return to the network. Furthermore, the user should be able to use the

Macintosh through the network as a terminal to the network's interactive computing facilities.

Finally, interacting with those facilities in the terminal-simulation mode, the user should be able to transfer a file from the network to those interactive computing facilities. As a result, existing time-sharing systems and personal computers will be able to use the services of the network, although not in the integrated transparent mode that may be possible for new workstations that can run the enhanced software. Finally, the new workstations should be able to run software environments that support applications developed in the most popular of the existing workstations. In particular, a program developed on either an IBM or IBM-compatible personal computer under IBM/MS-DOS or on a Macintosh should be run in a window on one of the more powerful new workstations that is fully integrated into the network.

The Role of Central Information Technology Service Units

The strength of higher education is derived largely from its decentralization and diversity. Since the new economics of information technology reinforce these institutional characteristics, diversity and decentralization will be fundamental to achieving our information technology goals. As a result, central activities need to be carefully targeted and designed so as to make the maximum amount of resources available to the various decentralized units in our colleges and universities. Therefore, while almost any information technology activity can, in principle, be accomplished through a central organization, the best organizational strategy for the future is based on quite the opposite premise. Information technology activities in higher education should be pursued at the lowest level of the organization consistent with their efficient and quality performance.

As a result, the majority of higher education investment in information technology will be distributed throughout the institution and investment in central service units will be tailored to maximize the return on the distributed investments made in the colleges and departments. The result is not a smaller or weaker set of central services, but a more strategic role for the central service units. The following strategic rationale justify investment in central facilities.

Scale Economies

In areas such as network support, software selection and maintenance, equipment maintenance and purchasing, a central organization can greatly increase a college or university's leverage and thereby make more effective use of financial and human resources.

Barriers to Entry

Some activities are either too large or require such close cooperation across the institution that they are difficult for any unit in the institution to support with its own resources. In particular, the provision of data networks, the purchase or mainframe computers and supercomputers, and the development of institutionwide systems software are not activities that can be accomplished through the independent efforts of distributed units within our colleges and universities.

Incentives in Support of Information Sharing

Colleges and universities are most fundamentally communities of scholars. If those communities are to prosper in the coming period where the information supporting scholarship is being increasingly found in electronic form, we must have a strategy that allows information to be shared both within the institutions and among the institutions. Even in those institutions with a tradition of high-quality support for information sharing, the advent of the desktop personal computer has led to a substantial decline in the coherence of the information technology environment.

Some industrial and commercial organizations attempt to maintain coherence through the promulgation and enforcement of standards regarding the type of workstations and software the users in the organization may choose. Such a standards-based coherence is not likely to be successful in the higher education environment because it contradicts the decentralized and diverse nature of the higher education enterprise and operates at cross-purposes to many of the values of academic freedom. As a result, coherence must be achieved in our scholarly community through incentives rather than through regulation.

Storage and exchange of information through a network and central file system must be easier than keeping it within the confines of a user's desktop machine. Such high-quality support and attractive pricing for strategic hardware and software products must be provided so these products become the obvious choice of single decision makers. Such high-quality interfaces to the universities' mainframes and supercomputers must be provided so people will use them rather than undertaking independent, duplicative systems efforts of their own. In short, centrally provided systems must motivate the units within our institutions and people within those units to make decisions that will lead to overall coherence of the information technology environment.

Equity

Equity of access across the institution is a critical goal. Access needs to be provided to students regardless of their ability to pay and to disciplines regardless of the state of technology development. We have information that indicates that students who come from less well-to-do backgrounds benefit more by access to instructional computing technology than do their more well-to-do peers. Major advances in many of the arts are now coupled to the use of sophisticated information technology, but the support for acquisition of that technology is much less available than in the sciences and engineering. The rapid improvement of price-performance in information technology means that leadership in a particular area often goes to those institutions able to afford the technology in its early stages before universal access becomes affordable.

Programs for placing large numbers of workstations in clusters around the campus and customizing those workstations to serve the various disciplines represent one major approach to addressing the equity problem. Other measures, such as the establishment of an institutionwide information technology access fee appropriately offset with financial aid, can make the technology available to all students, not just those who can easily afford it.

Efficiency

Finally, of course, capital must be invested where appropriate to increase the efficiency with which we perform other activities. While there are many opportunities, two areas stand out. A high-quality, effectively performing central staff with good interaction patterns throughout the institution can dramatically reduce the level of overall staffing required in the institution to support information technology. Second, investment in substantial mainframe computing capacity can provide for the use of more powerful development and information retrieval tools that increase the effectiveness with which people can use their time.

In summary, the critical strategic role of the central unit should be the stimulation of institutionally rational activities in decentralized areas and improvement of the efficiency and effectiveness of the overall institutions' ability to use information technology.

Prospects for Information Technology in Higher Education

What are the prospects for the use of information technology broadly throughout higher education? The economic and technological trends are abundantly clear. Information technology presents an overwhelming opportunity for higher education primarily because higher education as an industry is based on information—its creation and dissemination. Where information technology can be used effectively to support the missions of colleges and universities, it will become increasingly attractive over the coming years. Unfortunately, serious constraints operate to limit the introduction of this technology broadly throughout higher education.

Fundamentally, human and financial capital is inadequate. The development of applications to serve higher education is more expensive than individual institutions are able to afford and there is, as yet, no real market for such software throughout higher education. The workstations currently available fall short of the needs of higher education. Either the characteristics of the user interface are somewhat primitive or new applications are difficult to add to the system. Higher education is certainly not in a position to frequently reimplement the applications it develops. Furthermore, high-quality tools are crucial to implement new applications so they can be easily moved from one type of computing hardware to another.

The solutions to this lack of capital will require that we take advantage of trends already becoming visible. First, we will need to have a relatively low-price workstation available with sufficient power to support both a high quality user interface and a flexible development environment. A number of manufacturers appear to be ready to introduce such a workstation in 1987 at prices ranging from $3,000 to $6,000. Those workstations would be capable of running a fully implemented UNIX operating system with a high-quality, menu-driven, window-based user interface. They would have adequate memory and communications capability to fully support the networked environment outlined above.

Second, we will see a continuation of a trend toward shared investment to generate the financial capital required. That shared investment will probably proceed with the institutions making the investment in the central infrastructure and providing incentives for individuals to make investment in the workstations.

Third, the networked environment, which not only interconnects the workstations and servers within individual campuses but also provides linkages among campuses, will provide for straightforward transport of applications from one campus to another. A substantial market for high-quality applications for the higher education community may well result from such a networked environment.

All of this depends, of course, on convergence toward a few operating systems and user interfaces of a similar style. If we continue to proliferate operating system environments and user interfaces, a broad market will not emerge because development efforts will need to be duplicated for each environment.

Higher education will not be able to accomplish these objectives unless there is substantial interaction and cooperation with the information technology industry. There are points of mutual advantage to such a collaboration. Higher education requires products that push the technology frontiers and provides an environment in which innovation and change are welcome. As a result, higher education can provide a foundation for the development and testing of new technologies. Interaction can range from the close cooperation that characterized the Multics effort at MIT and the Information Technology Center at Carnegie-Mellon University to a much looser type of arrangement such as that supported in the IBM Advanced Education Projects and the Apple University Consortium.

As universities use advanced technology, they become a source for applications and software that can provide a broader vision of the technology's capabilities. Since most colleges and universities today have developed closer ties to the commercial and industrial environment, high-quality applications of information technology within the university can provide a showcase for the transfer of similar technology to the commercial and industrial marketplace. Furthermore, students go on into the commercial and industrial world and play a critical role in the development of new and advanced applications of information technology in that world. Their familiarity with the capabilities of the technology and the degree to which they are aware of its most advanced potentials has a substantial effect on the capability of the commercial and industrial market to absorb new uses of information technology.

In short, higher education should not be viewed or characterized as a niche market for the information technology industry, but should be understood as a leadership market. Successful applications of information technology in higher education will be a very powerful force for expansion of the overall information technology market.

Endnotes

1. Peter F. Drucker, *Managing for Results* (New York: Harper and Row, 1964); 5.

2 . These projections apply only to the electronic hardware, and not to computer programs and electromechanical devices such as printers.

3 . For more information, see "Grosch's Law," *Encyclopedia of Computer Science.* Anthony Ralston, ed. (New York: Petrocelli/Charter, 1976), 599.

4 . At the present time optical fibers are comparatively expensive to connect to devices that originate and/or receive information from them. Optical fibers are even more expensive to tap; that is, extract part of the information they carry without interrupting the other information carried on the light guide. As a result, optical fibers are now used primarily for high-capacity point-to-point communications and are rarely used to connect an individual device to a larger network. Over the coming decade, the problems of termination and tap cost will be addressed and the potential of optical fibers will be increasingly realized.

5 . This standard is only one of a family of competing IEEE 802 standards. Other standards include the IEEE 802.4 token-ring standard that is now being marketed by the IBM Corporation. Fortunately, networks based on different IEEE 802 standards can be interconnected via small computers that serve as "gateways" from one network to another.

6. A brief discussion of the various academic networks is presented in the Appendix of this paper.

7. The term refers to the second family of minicomputers from Digital Equipment Corporation, the VAX computers. They became as much a standard in scientific laboratories as IBM has become a standard in corporate data processing centers.

Appendix: A Summary of Academic Networks

General Purpose Networks

A number of these network initiatives are not linked to a particular disciplinary or regional perspective, but have either been the by-product of major federal initiatives or have sprung up as the result of voluntary confederations of university computing facilities.

ARPANET

ARPANET is the result of extensive funding for a networking experiment by the Department of Defense through the Advanced Research Projects Agency. While it was originally established to allow sharing of computing resources, ARPANET has contributed an enormous body of experience in network management, use patterns, and protocol development.

BITNET

EDUCOM has always been a major focal point for multi-university efforts. At present, EDUCOM provides the organizational home for BITNET and MAILNET, the two most broadly accessible interuniversity networks. BITNET started as a voluntary association of university computing organizations and is based on a store-and-forward network of leased lines utilizing protocols developed by the International Business Machines Corporation (IBM).

MAILNET

MAILNET is based on the use of technology developed for CSNET, which is limited to the Computer Science research community. MAILNET is based on a central hub placing switched circuit calls to all participating institutions to distribute and collect information. Since the central hub is at MIT, MAILNET has the capability of routing traffic through other networks when the nature of the traffic allows.

CCNET

CCNET is similar in philosophy to BITNET, but is based on Digital Equipment Corporation protocols. It is a smaller network that has a gateway to BITNET at Columbia University.

Disciplinary Networks

Several disciplinary networks have been established, the most important of which is CSNET, a network for the Computer Science research community. CSNET is built on the public packet-switching networks, leased lines, and switched circuit hub technology. It has numerous gateways to ARPANET, but is not similarly constrained regarding its users.

There are several other disciplinary networks in existence. Among the more notable are the National Magnetic Fusion Energy Computing Center network and the informal network established by the high energy experimental physics community. The National Center for Atmospheric Research (NCAR) is proposing to establish a network for the researchers who utilize its large-scale computing facilities and weather data.

Statewide Networks

The Merit network was one of the first networks to interconnect computing facilities at the major research universities in a state. It supports transport of data encapsulated in a variety of protocols. Merit provides reliable data transport for a large volume of traffic.

A number of other states have established networks, most of which tend to be more protocol-specific and less heavily used. Nonetheless, these networks typically provide extant points for user access at a large number of institutions. They can therefore provide an important means of expanding the reach of any new national network.

International Networks

Based on the BITNET experience, IBM has sponsored a similar network that spans much of Europe. The network is named the European Academic and Research Network (EARN). It is linked via multiple, leased circuits to BITNET.

Efforts are also underway to extend BITNET/EARN to the Middle East and Japan. As a result, the planning effort here proposed has the potential of providing international as well as United States access.

Library Networks

There are two service organizations that are playing an increasing role in providing college and university libraries with access to bibliographic and other related services. The Research Libraries Information Network (RLIN) is based at Stanford University in California and has an extensive array of leased telecommunications circuits. The OCLC Online Computer Library Center, Inc., is based in Dublin, Ohio and also has an extensive array of leased lines. Both organizations have a high level of interest in participating in a national higher education network.

University Summaries of Information Services and Activities

Brown University

The role of technology—particularly computing technology—in the creation, dissemination, and storage of information has increased sharply during the past decade. Brown is currently engaged in a major initiative to promote the creative use of advanced computing technologies. Brown wishes to help develop a powerful set of tools designed to enhance the scholarly work and day-to-day activities of faculty, students, and staff, and to understand how the use of such tools affects work and behavior. Brown's approach is to make tools broadly available in areas of scholarly endeavor where they prove effective.

Brown's organization to provide appropriate response to these needs includes the Libraries, Computing and Information Services (CIS), and the Institute for Research in Information and Scholarship (IRIS). The Libraries are internally automated and are developing an online system (BLIS) for a broadly accessible bibliographic record system as well as circulation and acquisition systems. CIS operates a campuswide network and services connected to that network. IRIS is engaged in experimentation on the use of technology in education and scholarly work, including the development of and aid in the installation of a Network of Scholar's Workstations.

As to progress, the Brown broadband cable system (BRUNET) was installed in 1981 and continues to provide excellent service interconnecting all buildings on campus, in order to carry terminal-to-mainframe data traffic, energy management and security system data, and television signals. In early 1986 there were 1700 ports attached to BRUNET. All major computer systems on campus are connected to it, and the telephone system is also connected to allow access by off-campus users. BRUNET is evolving as a high-speed (10 mbps) backbone service connecting a variety of local networks (Ethernets, AppleTalks, PCNets, etc.) which will also connect to external packet networks. Dormitories are wired with both broadband and AppleTalk connections among the rooms.

There are many computers using these facilities on and off campus. The Computer Center houses an IBM 3081 as its major system, as well as other smaller computers for specialized tasks (e.g., STAR, IBM 4381s, DEC 11/70). At many locations around the campus there are workstations of considerable power, manufactured by SUN, Apollo, Digital, Hewlett-Packard, IBM and others, in heavy use. About 2500 Apple Macintosh computers have been sold through the Brown Computer Store to faculty, students, and staff. IBM PCs and Apple Macintoshes are available to students and faculty in public centers, and there are 60 Apollo workstations in a classroom laboratory in active use almost around the clock. Much printing is done on centrally located Xerox laser printers or local laser printers from several manufacturers. Typesetting service is available via a phone link.

Enhancement of this environment is actively being pursued. InterNet is creating a hierarchical campus data network by connecting, via a high-speed, multi-channel broadband backbone, departmental networks using a variety of media and protocols. InterMedia is a project using advanced workstations, video and audio technologies in the classroom for instructional improvement, which is being tested in English, biology, and music classes. Networked IBM PC RTs are being installed in faculty offices and laboratories around the campus as part of the Network of Scholar's Workstations project. These projects were developed by IRIS and are being implemented with the cooperation of CIS, which will assume responsibility for their support beyond the testing phase. JOSIAH, the Library's online catalog, is being installed in cooperation with and under contract with Biblio-Techniques and is designed to be accessible from any point through the campus network. IRIS also has, as one of its major goals, a continuing study of the effect these technological changes have on the work going on and the people engaged in that work.

A new building to house the Computing and Information Services functions, classroom laboratories with workstations, the Department of Computer Science, and the Center for Scientific Computation is scheduled to be occupied in the early part of 1988.

References

Shipp, William S., Norman Meyrowitz, and Andries van Dam. "Networks of Scholars' Workstations in a University Community." In *Proceedings of the Twenty-Seventh IEEE Computer Society International Conference,* 108-22. Silver Spring, Md.: IEEE Computer Society Press, 1983.

Yankelovich, Nicole, Norman Meyrowitz, and Andries van Dam. "Reading and Writing the Electronic Book." *Computer* 18 (October 1985):15–29.

Young, Jeffrey S. "Hypermedia." *MacWorld* 3(March 1986):116–21.

Carnegie-Mellon University

Carnegie-Mellon is merging its libraries and computing into a single division of academic services. This will include libraries, computing, audiovisual, telecommunications, and classroom services. This is one of many changes being made to use the investment that the University has made over the past decade to create outstanding computing services. The center of these services is Andrew, a high-speed network of very powerful personal computers for everybody. This network is being developed in a joint project with IBM under the leadership of James H. Morris. The Andrew vision is that computing is carried out on personal computers, but data is stored on network file servers or database computers, such as the IBM mainframe which is used by the Library.

Libraries and Computing

The library of the future will provide access to books, journals, manuscripts, visual images, computers, machine-readable databases, services, and people. Faculty and students will come to the library, but much library information will also be available through the campus computing network. People will use books and they will use machine-readable text files. Demand for all types of information will undoubtedly increase.

The preferred personal computer on the network is an advanced function workstation running the Andrew enhancements to the UNIX operating system, but the network supports an enormous variety of computers and operating systems. A fundamental design requirement is that all of these can access the files, mail, and databases on the network. In this way, the libraries and computing are combining to provide campuswide service to the whole community.

The use of emerging technologies to provide access to information reemphasizes and, to a certain extent, redirects the traditional function of libraries. Computing technology provides new techniques for retrieving information, but the basic artifacts of information—books, journals, reports—have not changed drastically and will continue to predominate. The codex is a remarkable invention which has stood the test of time and will continue to be one of the primary forms of information distribution. The transition to the "electronic" book and journal will be gradual. The university already has the full text of a few scientific journals and reference works available in machine-readable form on large mainframe computers and optical disks.

Ten years ago the Carnegie-Mellon Libraries introduced remote database searching to the campus. Librarians have performed thousands of searches on DIALOG databases for faculty and students. The improved efficiency of identifying relevant journal citations has increased the demand for local resources and for resource-sharing arrangements with libraries throughout the region and the country. Technology is changing the *ways* in which people access information, resulting in an increased demand and need for information. The University is responding to the campus need for information by increasing the funds to purchase materials. In 1986/87, the budget for library materials will be 16 percent over 1985/86.

Library Databases

The Libraries maintain their internal database, the LS/2000 local library system, on a Data General computer housed in the Computing Center. The Libraries provide hardware, hardware and software maintenance, and database management. The LS/2000 system is available within the Libraries, and there is limited access over the campus network.

Public Databases and Retrieval System

The Libraries, the Computing Center, and the Information Technology Center are building a collection of public access databases on the University's IBM 3083 mainframe computer. The entire campus can access the Libraries' catalog on the IBM. Plans are under way to add high-use databases for journal literature. There is also considerable potential for databases containing information on Carnegie-Mellon faculty and staff, publications, working papers, and so forth.

Another area is the development of gateways to remote databases through the campus network. The Dow Jones Information Service and CompuServe are two databases proposed for campus access.

Numeric Databases

Numeric databases are a natural area of cooperation between libraries and computing. The Libraries pay the membership fee for the Interuniversity Consortium for Political and Social Research (ICPSR), an invaluable source for machine-readable data in the social sciences. The Libraries maintain the collection of printed guides and codebooks and are developing a machine-readable directory of ICPSR resources. Academic Computing provides consultation and software support for manipulating data.

Educational Computing

The decentralization of academic computing and the widespread use of personal computers have created a major new task: to collect, catalog, publicize, and distribute information about software and other course materials. This is being tackled jointly by the Libraries, the Center for Design of Educational Computing, and the Interuniversity Consortium for Educational Computing. The underlying methodology is to adapt traditional librarianship to this new field.

Massachusetts Institute of Technology

At the Massachusetts Institute of Technology (MIT), as at other institutions, professional workstations are becoming the dominant computing resource for most users, although demand for access to more powerful machines and to central files and expertise continues.

Information Systems

MIT, in 1984, reorganized its computer resources to adjust to these changing needs. The resulting Information Systems group provides computing services for academic and administrative use, telecommunications ranging from telephone service to campuswide computer and cable television networks, and support services for the full range of information technology available at MIT. Each of the group's four subdivisions has a distinct set of responsibilities; the four units are strongly linked to assure quality, efficiency, and consistency across the spectrum of computing resources.

Information Services holds primary responsibility for educating, training, and assisting current and prospective computer users, providing courses and seminars, consultation and documentation. The staff serves as a clearinghouse for information on other computing resources within the Institute and is responsible for obtaining site licenses for widely used software.

The Microcomputer Center provides sales and consulting on personal computers and professional workstations and related software. The Center's goal is to help members of the MIT community acquire and effectively use microcomputer technology. The Center provides substantial discounts on equipment, evaluates software, offers consultation on technical problems and maintenance, and maintains a library of microcomputer information and software.

Administrative Systems sets standards and procedures for acquiring, developing, and maintaining software and databases to be used in the Institute's administrative offices. Teams of programmers, service, and documentation specialists are available to work with staff in administrative areas to solve their computing needs.

Telecommunications Systems is responsible for developing, installing, and maintaining the campuswide network to transport messages between workstations, file servers, mainframes, and other resources. They have also contracted for and will oversee the installation of an AT&T 5ESS telephone system which will transport voice, data, and video.

Project Athena

MIT's Project Athena is a five-year experiment in educational computing to help the Institute and its industrial sponsors, DEC and IBM, better understand the potential of networked, high-performance personal computing in the university's curriculum. Project Athena is in its third year at MIT and is now the most widely used educational computing facility on campus, providing computational services for educational purposes to all undergraduates and faculty at MIT. Athena is used in about fifty courses, with a combined enrollment of over 2000.

The current configuration is a network of time-sharing VAXs and PC ATs used in a workstation format. Over the next three years, there will be a massive transition from the time-sharing environment to workstations which are "individual" computers with advanced graphics capabilities and six times the current computing power. Present installations are in clusters in academic buildings and libraries. A phased installation of workstations into living groups is under way. The goal is to have workstations in all student dormitories and independent living groups. For installation and maintenance of its workstations, Athena contracts with units of Information Systems, and the networking being done for Athena is part of the greater MIT networking plan.

It is not yet certain how many Athena workstations there will be. The best guess is between 1500 and 2000 "ports," or places for members of the MIT community to work. There are currently about 600 ports, divided evenly between DEC and IBM facilities. For the question, What happens after Athena? the answer is not yet known. Options range from abandoning the idea of computing as an integral part of an MIT education to the further expansion of computing so that each member of the community has his or her own workstation. For the remainder of the Project, MIT will continue to study the ways that Athena has affected the educational process at MIT.

The MIT Libraries

The Libraries collect information and provide services to support research and teaching at MIT. The collection of 2 million printed volumes, 20,000 current subscriptions, and extensive other holdings includes books, journals, conference proceedings, microforms, videotapes, machine-readable data, and digital and audio disks. The collections and staff are decentralized, being housed in five major and several minor locations, each unit being in reasonable proximity to its major user population.

The Libraries use information technology for cataloging materials, for providing access to abstracts and indexes in reference service, for communicating with other libraries to borrow materials for MIT users, for support of internal accounting and managerial functions, and for circulation and public access to the Libraries' catalog. The online circulation and public access system, Barton, is currently being implemented.

It has a database of over 300,000 items and supports about 40 (ultimately 150) terminals.

Future plans for the application of technology to the provision of library and information services fall into four categories: (1) the conversion of local manual files to online ones; (2) the possible purchase on optical digital disk of files currently accessed remotely and publications currently received in print form; (3) the replacement of dumb terminals being used for some applications with intelligent workstations; and (4) the linking of the Libraries' online files and human resources to the Institute community through the campus network. Each of these is in a different stage of development—some are being implemented, others are in experimental stages, and still others are now under investigation.

University of California, San Diego

The University of California, San Diego (UCSD) is actively planning for the provision of information resources for its campus and public communities. Campus information resources have been identified, an appropriate organization is in place, the installation of a local area network is nearly completed, an academic computing plan is under development, and library automation planning and development are well along. The campus is developing a long-range academic plan which will be the major integrating force for information resource planning.

Campus Information Resources

The *University Library* includes the Central University Library, the Biomedical Library, Scripps Institution of Oceanography Library, the Science and Engineering Library, the Slide and Photograph Collection, and the Undergraduate Library. Book collections total 1,700,000; there are 31,000 active serial subscriptions; special collections in music, government documents, machine-readable data files, rare books and manuscripts, and maps supplement the general stack collections.

The *Office of Academic Computing (OAC)* includes the Academic Computing Center, the Academic Computing Services Office, and Academic Network Operations. The Academic Computing Center maintains eight minicomputers and several hundred public access terminals for instruction and the Remote User Access Center for campus access to the San Diego Supercomputer Center. It also maintains five minicomputers for general recharge computing for sponsored faculty research and for departmental word processing. Academic Network Operations maintains an Ungermann-Bass Local Area Network (campus) which provides terminal service to most academic computers on campus and also provides internet communications between building or departmental networks. At present 2200 terminal connections exist on the UCSD Local Area Network.

The *San Diego Supercomputer Center* was established by the National Science Foundation to provide supercomputer services to scientists in the United States. This facility is managed by G. A. Technologies on the UCSD campus. Both UCSD's upper campus (general campus and School of Medicine) and the lower campus (Scripps Institution of Oceanography) are charter consortium members of the San Diego Supercomputer Center. As such, they each have 200 Cray XMP processor hours per year to use for educational and interdisciplinary or innovative research activity beyond the time that is awarded by the Center or by the National Science Foundation to individual researchers.

The *Media Center* is responsible for the production and presentation of television and video for classroom use. Faculty data files result from and are used for individual research projects.

Public Information Offices in the School of Medicine, Scripps Institution of Oceanography, and on the general campus provide information to the general public.

The *Office of Contracts and Grants* maintains files on faculty research interests and publications.

The *Office of Learning Resources, School of Medicine,* is responsible for audiovisual and microcomputer support for teaching and research in the School of Medicine.

Organization

The two key agencies for developing campus information resources, the University Library and the Office of Academic Computing, report to the

Vice Chancellor-Academic Affairs. The joint reporting line facilitates the cooperative efforts under way.

New Technologies on Campus

The University of California, San Diego campus, is making extensive use of computers in most academic departments. Recently developed departmental academic computing plans have identified computing resources needed for teaching and research, and implementation of those plans has begun. The goal is to provide all faculty with a computer workstation and to replace these on a five-year schedule to avoid obsolescence. A second goal is to provide all faculty with access to the Local Area Network; first as a device for terminal service and later as a device for file, print, database, and other types of services.

Departments are required to submit an annual academic computing plan for review. This document serves as the starting point for justifying departmental budget requests for instructional computing equipment and for central computing center services. This document also serves as an input into the general campus academic planning document. The Office of Academic Computing solicits these plans and consolidates them into the annual campus plan for academic computing. This office also advises the Vice Chancellor-Academic Affairs and the divisional deans about the budgetary implications of such plans. Finally, the Office of Academic Computing provides the departments with technical assistance in the preparation of these plans.

Academic Computing Services is assembling a "library" of public domain software. This will reside on the management machine for the campus Local Area Network and be operated in the manner of a bulletin board. Programs for all popular microcomputers will be provided with the emphasis on programs for MS-DOS systems and the Apple Macintosh. Reviews of commercial software and campus publications about academic computing will also be provided as part of this service. The service is expected to be available this summer [1986].

The University of California San Diego Library is a heavy user of the University of California MELVYL online union catalog, although the MELVYL development is not yet a total replacement for the card catalog. The Library and the Office of Academic Computing are working to make MELVYL available over the Local Area Network so that the resources of the University of California library system can be accessed by any terminal on campus. A local online catalog with associated catalog maintenance and circulation systems is under development on a contract with Biblio-Techniques; a decision on an automated serials control and acquisition system is imminent. The Biomedical Library is prototyping an electronic-mail-based service for asking reference questions, renewing books, and ordering photocopies of journal articles. If successful, the service will be extended to the rest of the campus community.

Most of the Library's reference staff are trained in online searching and do computer-based reference searches routinely. The Library also provides a variety of training programs in online searching for end users, including one-on-one training in the use of MELVYL, classroom training on MELVYL, and an eight-hour course in Medline searching which entitles its graduates to a Medline password.

In the area of joint information service programs, the Library and OAC have contributed to a faculty proposal for the joint management of a Social Science Data Service and are working with a faculty research committee on the development of a faculty research database for the campus.

References

Advisory Committee on Preservation. Subcommittee C. (John Mallinson, Chair). *Strategic Technology Considerations Relative to the Preservation and Storage of Human and Machine Readable Records: White paper.* Prepared for the National Archives and Records Service, July 1984.

King, Kenneth M. "Evolution of the Concept of Computer Literacy." *EDUCOM Bulletin* 20 (Fall 1985):18–21.

Library Trends (Winter 1982). Entire issue devoted to "Data Libraries for the Social Sciences." See especially articles by Margaret O'Neill Adams, Ray Jones, Laine G. M. Ruus, and Alice Robbin.

Mallinson, John. "Archiving Human and Machine Readable Records for the Millenium." To be published shortly in *ARCHIVARIA* (Journal of the Association of Canadian Archivists).

Neff, Raymond K. "Merging Libraries and Computer Centers: Manifest Destiny or Manifestly Deranged?" *EDUCOM Bulletin* 20 (Winter 1985):8–12, 16.

University of Edinburgh

It has long been University policy to link Library, administrative and academic computers (departmental as well as central) on a single campuswide network. That network is linked in turn to the Joint Academic Network (Janet) which interconnects all universities and many other institutions of higher education and research in the United Kingdom (UK) and has gateways to European research networks, to national and international packet-switched services, and to Darpanet and the UNIX network.

The University is scattered over a considerable part of Edinburgh and the main network is a wide-area type like Telenet, with gateways to departmental and other local area networks. The expectation is that the number and variety of departmental networks will increase considerably and a major objective is to ensure adequate interlinking capabilities. The network extends into student residences but not into individual student rooms.

The University has greatly benefitted, as have other universities and institutes in the United Kingdom, from the existence of a nationally funded Computer Board. The Board provides funds for some aspects of university computing, but, more important, has funded and encouraged internetworking between institutions, and in particular has established interim national protocol standards in the absence of agreed international ones. As a result, electronic mail and file transfer are heavily used in the academic community and embrace a wide range of hardware and systems. Organizationally, the Library and the administrative and academic computing services are autonomous but close liaison exists and there is a considerable amount of cross-representation in the membership of committees. All departments with an interest in information technology are represented on an IT Committee which includes representatives from agencies (such as Hewlett-Packard) from outside the University.

Undergraduate Computing Needs

Most undergraduate computing takes place on central services or departmental machines, partly for reasons of cost (particularly of software) but also because of the file management problems which arise with a multiplicity of micros. However, the use of personal workstations is growing rapidly and most students arrive with experience gained at school and often at home. There is a growing interest in several Social Sciences Departments in the development of shared large-scale databases (for example, of financial and economic indicators). These will be held on a central machine from which students and teachers will extract appropriate subsets for classroom use. The University is also actively engaged in developing for certain disciplines user-friendly software to enable the relatively naive student to explore complex databases without the need to learn any formal programming.

Administration

The University Secretary's Office is making increasing use of the Edinburgh Computing Network (Ednet) for the transmission of student records, calendars, and other administrative documents. A new student record system has recently been implemented which will store a wide range of information about a student's present and past academic history. Subject to stringent security requirements, this system is being developed to provide information across the varied administrative units of the University. In a scattered University, in which much administration and decision making are devolved to Faculties, this is a particular advantage.

The Library

The Library is the most traditional of the agencies in the University involved in information transfer. Its peculiar role is to provide access not only to the latest research data of particular importance to scientists and social scientists, but also to works of art and literature and to the thinking of the past. The collections, accrued over four centuries, are scattered over many sites, and until recently awareness and access for all members of the University to the dispersed holdings were difficult. The Library sees the advent of networked systems as its salvation not only for more efficient administration but also for more effective use of its resources by readers.

The Library has engaged on a project, EULOGIA (Edinburgh University Library Online for General Information Access), to provide an online information service throughout the University, and indeed beyond, through Janet and other national networks. At the core of this service lies the database currently mounted on a Geac 8000 computer system which is a host on the University network. Since most information required for study and research is still locked up in books and journals, the Library is giving priority to the retroconversion of its catalogs. The first phase covers the conversion of the records, hitherto of varying bibliographic standard, physical form and presentation, to one standard (UK MARC, AACR2) format within 7.5 years; after three years about 25% of the work has been done. This phase covers the records for 1.5 million books and journals.

When the immediate goal has been reached, the Library will turn to the networking of information on other academic resources both within its own collections (archives, manuscripts, press-cuttings, maps,

audiovisual materials, machine-readable data files) and in other parts of
the University (such as the slide collection of the Fine Art Department,
the dialect recordings of the School of Scottish Studies, the harpsichord
collection of the Faculty of Music). The aim will be to provide as comprehensive a picture as possible of the materials of scholarship and science
and to make them known to the academic community at large.

Material from EULOGIA is not merely viewed on the screen, but may
be downloaded for use in theses and lectures, printed out as reading lists,
passed to other libraries for their own purposes, and used as a basis for
interlibrary loans and cooperative conservation policies.

EULOGIA also provides the enquirer from any part of the University with directory information on Library opening hours, facilities, ex-
hibitions, seminars, and special events. It includes an online accessions
list covering a rolling nine-week period and a union list of over 20,000
serials currently received in Edinburgh libraries. EULOGIA also offers access through Janet to other libraries and to commercial databases. It has
an online suggestions box for comments which, together with system
logs, brings ample evidence that the Library's online services are meeting
a growing need.

Data Libraries and Data Archives

A special feature of the University of Edinburgh was its pioneering role
in the provision of data library services, brought about through the collaboration of the University Library with the applications section of the
University's computing services. A wide range of statistical material (including small area census statistics) may be accessed over the network
directly from the University's mainframe computers using specially
developed software which includes facilities for the direct mapping of
results. A parallel development has involved the establishment of the Scottish Education Data Archive which provides access to data from a long
series of surveys of Scottish Secondary pupils; this database is used as a
research resource not only within the University but also by a wide range
of educational policy makers (including Central Government) in Scotland.

University of Illinois at
Urbana-Champaign

As befits a decentralized campus, the University of Illinois at Urbana-
Champaign has relied on a number of agencies to both identify and address the information needs of the campus. The campus is a participant
in information systems sponsored and administered by the general

university, such as personnel and accounting systems, and it provides campus agencies, such as the University Library and the Academic Computer Center. The University of Illinois at Urbana-Champaign also participates in a series of information networks appropriate not only to itself as a campus but to the individual academic components. That is, information needs in the College of Commerce are served not only by the system and institution provided through the campus of the university but through the disciplinary networks that the college participates in.

It is recognized that a campus and university of this size and complexity are unlikely to be served by a single policy-making and administrative person or body. It is the university's opinion the best policy is for each college and academic unit to address and develop the information networks that it needs using its own, campus, and university resources.

The university is committed to and actively engaging in rewiring the campus to provide the communications technologies over which information can be sent and received. This rewiring is to provide both a voice-grade and a data network as well as its own locally owned telephone system. The system is designed to allow local area networks to be designed throughout the institution without having to provide further wiring.

The *Campus Research Computer Center* serves as an information resource as well as a processing center. It is under the aegis of the Computer Center that such questions as privacy of files, and other related topics are discussed and policies are recommended to the campus when such are appropriate. The Director of the Campus Research Computer Center serves the campus as an expert in such areas and is often called upon to comment on policies, problems, services, and techniques which are being developed by the general university computing and information divisions.

The *University Library* is an information resource which is both extensive and highly decentralized. It provides not only traditional library materials but certainly has been making beginning steps into the acquisition of library materials in such formats as CD-ROM and similar machine-readable data formats. The Senate Library Committee which not only counsels and oversees the Library's activities also has engaged in a series of discussions about the Library's role in the provision and acceptance of machine-readable data and looks toward resolving those issues. In each college there has arisen to one degree or another some form of information processing capability. In the Colleges of Engineering and Commerce that ability is well developed and each of them runs what amounts to computer centers, either a smaller scale mainframe computer itself or a center using mini- and microcomputers. One should note that the College of Engineering has been designated a national center for supercomputing and a national center for compound semiconductor microelectronics. It furthermore has received support to develop another generation of supercomputers.

All of these activities have some effect on information policy. One also should be cognizant that there are research activities in this field being carried on by a number of campus units. The Coordinated Science Laboratory, a division of the College of Engineering, the Graduate School of Library and Information Science, the Computer Science Department, the Department of Electrical Engineering, and the College of Communications all do research in the fields of information policies and processing.

Thus from the Department of English, which is now using personal computers on a pilot and experimental basis to give instruction in freshman composition and rhetoric, to the College of Agriculture, which uses complex microcomputer-based information gathering systems on the food intake and weight gain of farm animals, to the science departments of the College of Liberal Arts and Sciences, which use computation and machine-based information as a standard tool in the pursuit of their disciplines, there is a continued interest in a decentralized approach to information as both a commodity, a process, and an end in itself.

University of Toronto

The University of Toronto Computer Services (UTCS) 1986/87 plan is an ambitious one that involves virtually every aspect of the University. It is briefly summarized below, but it should be recognized that not all of the plans have been funded, and some may not be funded to the level necessary to carry out the intended mission.

A major Facility Management initiative will be the operation and support of the supercomputer which has resulted in two major activities: the ongoing introduction of a new VM/CMS academic service and, on the administrative computer, the conversion from the MVS operating system and IMS database system to MVS/XA and a new database system DB2. The university will continue to extend the backbone communications network.

The Ideal Computing/Communication Situation

The ideal computing communications situation for the University has at least three components: (1) a pervasive, high bandwidth value-added network supporting academic and administrative needs, (2) adequate processing, data storage and input/output capacity, and (3) a broad range of services easily accessible over the network. Within this environment, the principal mandate of UTCS is to plan, implement, and operate central computer facilities and common-carrier data networks and to plan and support divisional, departmental or project computer facilities. The focus of the UTCS effort will not be on the development of systems but on the implementation and integration of systems defined on the basis of academic or administrative needs.

UTCS will become increasingly involved in the expansion of telecommunication services on campus as a provider of common-carrier services. Additional resources will be needed to provide microcomputer support services that are consistent with changing patterns of machine ownership and directions in academic computing. A number of facilities are likely to be specifically, but not necessarily uniquely, provided and supported because of their high cost to divisional units. These might include supercomputing services, large-scale data storage and staging, high-quality print or graphics devices, fourth generation languages, scanners, some public databases and tape storage and retrieval. These directions mark a shift from UTCS's being primarily an operator of large central machines to an increased emphasis on facilities management and networking.

UTCS currently provides Facility Management services to seven facilities:

1. Computing Disciplines Facility (VAX-based) provides instructional computing to upper-level computing science students.

2. Computing Disciplines Facility (PC-based) provides computing resources to lower-level computer science students through ninety-five microcomputers in five locations, most connected to local area networks that are in turn interconnected.

3. Economics Policy Analysis and Sociology Facility delivers VM/CMS services to the three named departments.

4. Institutional Relations Facility provides the Department of Private Funding and the Department of Alumni Affairs with access to databases for fund-raising purposes.

5. Statistics Consulting Service.

6. & 7. Erindale College and Scarborough College Computer Centres which provide undergraduate computing resources.

In addition, the Centre for Computing in the Humanities is expected to commence operation in fiscal year 1986/87. Current plans call for several on-campus sites housing personal computers on local networks, terminals, and related equipment supporting teaching and research in the humanities. Finally, the Department of Mechanical Engineering has approached IBM concerning a cooperative venture in CADCAM. UTCS would propose a Facility Management service for such an operation.

Microcomputer Services

Thusfar, microcomputer support personnel have been limited by the hardware and software obtained as gifts or loans or through discretionary funds. It has been recommended that a continuing fund be established as a Software Library and Hardware Renewal Fund.

The Statistics and Numerical Analysis Computing group has been evaluating a component called RLINK that facilitates interaction between a micro and a mainframe and requires high-speed dial-in modems or dedicated links to UTCS facilities. UTCS hopes to facilitate access by establishing a pool of modems that could be rented to users.

UTCS wishes to expand its maintenance capabilities to include not only the IBM PCs and PC XTs, but also the IBM PC AT and some compatibles, as well.

In the past several years many users have incorporated the use of personal computers into their production of text. Generally these people continue to use mainframe computers in conjunction with their microcomputers. UTCS has been lagging behind the user community it supports and recommends that steps be taken to remedy this.

Imaging Support

There has long been a requirement to merge computer-generated graphics and text to form a single image. There are now several hardware and software products that perform the task affordably. These products also serve to bridge the gap between inexpensive computer images and high-quality typesetting. Such products will allow UTCS to deliver an enhanced service and provide an alternative to the obsolete typesetting currently in service.

Affordable laser printers should be installed wherever it makes sense. The devices chosen should be PostScript-compatible so that they may also be used as graphic output devices and pseudo-typesetters. They should be networked to existing mainframes, so that with the existing web of inter-connections with other campus mainframes, they could act as plot servers to users in their immediate vicinity and switched to local mini- or microcomputers, if connectivity were maintained. UTCS is proposing the acquisition of this device as a central resource and also that a microcomputer be obtained to support not only this service but imaging in general.

University of Toronto Networking

As a consequence of the diversity of solutions to computing needs and the extent to which the campus is distributed, no single technology solution will likely apply. A number of trends are observed:

- More computing is occurring.
- Computing is increasingly performed on departmental or faculty facilities.
- The requirements for access to computing from any part of the campus is increasing.
- Cross appointments and joint projects result in demands for computer-to-computer and terminal-to-computer data flows.
- Electronic messaging is becoming a normal and expected method of dialogue within or external to the University.

In addition, when users of computing experience high-performance communications, their perceptual view is changed, even when the same application functions are provided.

Infrastructure Investments

The University's installation of a copper and fibre optic cable plant is an example of an investment in the infrastructure necessary to support past and present initiatives. This plant is already providing substantial benefits to (1) the instructional programs of the Department of Computer Science, (2) the production applications of the University administrations, and (3) the research endeavors of the Institute for Policy Analysis. These facilities have allowed the development of an embryonic campus communications backbone. It is proposed to extend the existing physical infrastructure and provide for additional initiatives which should be regraded as infrastructure investments.

Campus Backbone

A campus communications backbone is the digital highway intercon-necting various computing and communications domains within the cam-pus. As such, it needs to be independent of the meaning of the data that are carried on it. It is required to cater to increasing demands for traffic capacity over a period of perhaps twenty years. The backbone is to carry that traffic destined to be crossing building or building complex physical boundaries. Another function that can be provided by a backbone archi-tecture is the isolation of private domains that may be necessary due to load or security concerns.

The initiatives to date have identified optical fibre as the key physical transport medium for the backbone. At this time the backbone is implemented as a common Ethernet operating over optical fibre, but the existing Ethernet backbone has reached the specification timing limits. A primary advantage of Ethernet is the plentiful supply of products and services that can be used to satisfy demands, but the capacity of an Ethernet is insufficient over the long term for a campus backbone.

NETNORTH Evolution

In 1984, UTCS agreed to participate on a trial basis for one year in the then fledgling Ontario Universities VM Network. The architecture and implementation of this network were patterned after the existing United States BITNET. The networks operate on a store-and-forward basis which requires each VM environment to be responsible for traffic to other universities. One of the costs of this network is for Bell data communica-tions facilities. The network, now called NETNORTH, has become suc-cessful and offers almost worldwide connectivity and has proven valuable to both academic and administrative members of the University.

Supercomputer Access

The impending arrival of a Cray Supercomputer at the University requires that methods of communicating jobs and data to it be examined. Access to the Cray from an IBM environment is most easily accomplished through the existing VM system. This system, coupled with the 3088 MCCU and Channel Extenders can provide high-speed access to the Cray from any on-campus IBM machine. Off-campus access can be provided via the facilities of NETNORTH.

Administrative Enhancements

Implementation of the Fibre Optic-based Channel Extenders has produced significant qualitative and quantitative benefits. In those buildings where a need to access the administrative system exists, access to an IBM channel would be desirable. At this time it appears that such concentration occurs in Simcoe Hall and Robarts Library.

Electronic Messaging

It is proposed that UTCS implement a micro VAX-based X400 message system for all suitable campus computers.

The Library

The University and the library hope that in 1986/87 the implementation of an automated circulation/inquiry system will finally become a reality by the purchase of the UTLAS T/Series 50 System, which will provide a full circulation system, including the inquiry function as an integrated system that allows for public access via either terminals or IBM PCs. The public access catalogue would be available in all locations either through a terminal (initially in the Central Library) or by IBM PCs in other locations, with later possibility of connection via terminals or other personal computers located in any site, including faculty homes and offices. Initially a total of 100 terminals will be installed, but the computer hardware has capacity for future expansion.

Vanderbilt University

Vanderbilt is making significant investments in its information services. Its goal is to be an early adopter of proven technologies, and on occasion, to accept the risks of experimentation with untested systems. It views the important limits on the adoption of new technologies as cultural and managerial rather than technological or financial. Therefore, the university insists that the faculty lead the way with curricular innovations and with the adoption of new systems for research. The university expects everyone in the community to become more sophisticated about computing and to make sensible decisions about computing. An environment with decisions being made by thousands of people can only be coherent if prices are used aggressively to manage the diverse resources. The university will employ price incentives to shape behavior appropriately while encouraging the growth of computing.

The program of investments in electronic systems includes:

1. Library Systems: Acorn
2. Data Communications Facilities: Caravan
3. Distributed Computer Systems
4. Hub Computer Services
5. Personal Workstations

The Heard Library implemented an integrated library automation system called Acorn in 1985. It uses Northwestern's NOTIS software running on an IBM 4361 owned by the Library but located in and managed by the Computer Center. Two-thirds of the Library's holdings are now in the system and 90 percent should be included by the end of 1986. The system encompasses all seven libraries including law and medical and supports 120 terminals. Circulation using barcodes affixed to the books began in January 1986 and the acquisitions module with fund accounting and serials control will begin later in 1986. Acorn services are available on the data communications network.

The Heard Library has received a grant from the Pew Memorial Trust to extend the range of information available electronically. It contemplates bringing such article citation files as Medline, ERIC, and PsycINFO to campus perhaps on compact disks. It is also interested in the possibility of distributing full text documents with graphics in electronic form. It is committed to delivery to the desktop when practical. The Library is likely to expand its purchase of print materials somewhat, but hopes for some substitution in acquisition and some consequent savings in space in the future.

The plan is to have a campuswide backbone network called Caravan. A prototype broadband is installed from the Computer Center to two engineering buildings and additional legs are at the proposal stage. To this point, the DECNET protocol is being used for communication, but other protocols are expected to be used as well, raising protocol conversion issues. Inside buildings, Caravan bridges to Ethernets that can support terminal servers, local Ethernet connections, and links to AppleTalk and other local systems.

In August, the university will switch over from the Northern Telecom telephone switches to a NEAX 2400 switch supporting 15,000 lines with significant growth potential. The NEAX 2400 will support data traffic at 9600 bps or better and is appropriate for low-speed and low-traffic locations. The relative places of the digital PBX and of the broadband service are expected to sort themselves out over time and in response to changing relative prices. There will be a digital interface between the NEAX and Caravan.

The university encourages the growth of distributed computer systems. Economies of scale in computing have diminished so that the economies of specialization and managerial control dominate. The university expects to acquire systems that are optimized for particular applications, and that are managed to the benefit of the unit most affected. The Computer Center provides a facilities management service on a contract basis with schools, departments, and the Library, and it expects to add more such arrangements. In addition, several research groups have their own facilities. The expectation is that the availability of high-quality data communication services via Caravan will create the desired degree of connectivity and compatibility.

Three important roles are envisioned for Hub Computer Services to allow the university to take advantage of economies of scale where they remain. The first role is as a communications hub, providing electronic mail, file servers both private and public, and access to off-campus services. The second role is the provision of larger scale computing primarily for computer-bound jobs. Computing in the supercomputing class is expected to be done off campus and will provide communications and user support for off-campus service. There is a niche between the departmental machine and the supercomputer to be filled by the hub. The third role is in planning, system development, and design, a service of value throughout the computing environment and relatively independent of hardware.

The university has had a tri-processor DEC 10 as the general purpose mainframe and is now seeking follow-on equipment. The choice of follow-on gear will be different in several respects from what has come before. The university plans to expand capacity gradually as demand requires rather than making less frequent major financial commitments. In this way, it can more quickly respond to new technological developments and maintain flexibility in balancing distributed versus hub resources. In addition, different units at the hub may be optimized for particular tasks. The first decision about new hub equipment should be made by June [1986]. Hub Services will carry prices for current use that will improve the quality of service provided and induce thoughtful choice about alternative ways of completing computing tasks.

The university supports purchase of microcomputers by faculty. The College of Arts and Science offers financial support for faculty purchases when a faculty member proposes significant integration of computing into a course. The Engineering and Management Schools have also supported faculty purchases. The university expects to see a growing penetration of computer use in the curriculum. When the penetration becomes significant, it will begin to encourage students to buy personal equipment. It expects to provide effective data communications services to dorm rooms. The investment required for individual student ownership with communication capability may well be near $2,500 per student, roughly 3 percent of the total cost of a four-year education. The university wants assurance that such an investment will yield significant educational dividends before it is launched.

Vanderbilt University has ambitious plans. It has made some important moves. It avoids risk when it can. It looks for ways to make gains at modest cost. The university would like to take advantage of well-supported products and to learn from the experience of others. It is enthusiastic about the prospects for improving the productivity of intellectual pursuits by using electronic systems.

Appendixes

Appendix A Higher Education Policy Advisory Committee to OCLC

The Higher Education Policy Advisory Committee to OCLC was formed to help guide OCLC in the direction of its research, the allocation of its resources, and the emphasis of its efforts in the service of higher education. The Committee's discussions and deliberations are far-ranging. Following is a list of members:

Richard C. Atkinson
Chancellor
University of California, San Diego
LaJolla, California 92093

Richard M. Cyert
President
Carnegie-Mellon University
5000 Forbes Avenue
Pittsburgh, Pennsylvania 15213

Maurice Glicksman
Provost and Dean of Faculty
Box 1862
University Hall
Brown University
Providence, Rhode Island 02912

Oscar Handlin
Carl M. Loeb University Professor
Widener Library
Room 783
Harvard University
Cambridge, Massachusetts 02138

Alexander Heard
Chancellor Emeritus and
  Professor of Political Science
Vanderbilt University
Institute for Public Policy Studies
1801 Edgehill Avenue
Nashville, Tennessee 37212

Robert M. O'Neil
President
University of Virginia
Madison Hall
P. O. Box 9011
Charlottesville, Virginia 22906-9011

Anne Firor Scott
Center for Advanced Study in the
  Behavioral Sciences
202 Junipero Serra Boulevard
Stanford, California 94305

Adele S. Simmons
President
Hampshire College
Amherst, Massachusetts 01002

Sir Peter Swinnerton-Dyer FRS
Chairman
University Grants Committee
14, Park Crescent
London W1N 4DH
ENGLAND

Clarence L. Ver Steeg
Dean of The Graduate School
Northwestern University
633 Clark Street
Evanston, Illinois 60201

Appendix B Participants

Institutional Participants

Brown University
    Maurice Glicksman, Provost
    Brian Hawkins, Vice President for Computer and Information Services
    Martha E. Schaffer, Assistant Professor, Hispanic and Italian Studies
    Howard R. Swearer, President
    Merrily E. Taylor, Director of Libraries

Carnegie-Mellon University
    William Arms, Vice President of Computing and Information Services
    John P. Crecine, Senior Vice President for Academic Affairs
    Richard M. Cyert, President
    Thomas J. Michalak, Director of University Libraries

Massachusetts Institute of Technology
    James D. Bruce, Director of Information Systems
    Paul E. Gray, President
    Jay K. Lucker, Director of Libraries

University of California, San Diego
    Donald W. Anderson, Director, Office of Academic Computing
    Richard C. Atkinson, Chancellor
    Dorothy Gregor, University Librarian
    Gary C. Jacobson, Professor, Department of Political Science
    Harold K. Ticho, Vice Chancellor for Academic Affairs

University of Edinburgh
    Michael Anderson, Department of Economic History and Dean of the Faculty
        of Social Sciences
    John H. Burnett, Principal and Vice Chancellor
    Brenda E. Moon, University Librarian
    Peter E. Williams, Acting Director of the Edinburgh Regional Computing
        Centre

University of Illinois at Urbana-Champaign
    Hugh C. Atkinson, University Librarian
    George F. Badger, Jr., Director, Computing Services Office
    Leigh S. Estabrook, Dean, Graduate School of Library and Information Science
    Thomas E. Everhart, Chancellor

University of Toronto
  George E. Connell, President
  Joan E. Foley, Vice President and Provost
  R. J. Helmstadter, Professor of History, Chairman, Library Advisory Committee
  Allan Heyworth, Coordinator of Telecommunications and Computer Networks
  Carole R. Moore, Chief Librarian

Vanderbilt University
  Malcolm Getz, Director of Libraries
  Charles A. Kiesler, Provost
  Joe B. Wyatt, Chancellor

Individual Participants

  Evelyn Daniel, Dean, School of Library Science, The University of North Carolina at Chapel Hill
  Shirley Echelman, Executive Director, Association of Research Libraries
  Warren J. Haas, President, Council on Library Resources
  Robert M. Hayes, Dean, Graduate School of Library and Information Science, University of California, Los Angeles
  Robert M. O'Neil, President, University of Virginia
  Anne Firor Scott, W. K. Boyd Professor, Duke University
  Douglas E. Van Houweling, Vice Provost for Information Technology, University of Michigan
  Clarence L. Ver Steeg, Dean, The Graduate School, Northwestern University

The Johnson Foundation Participants

  William B. Boyd, President
  Henry Halstead, Vice President

OCLC Participants

  Rowland C. W. Brown, President and Chief Executive Officer
  Mary Ellen Jacob, Vice President, Library Planning
  Michael J. McGill, Vice President, Research and Technical Planning
  H. Paul Schrank, Jr., Vice President, Membership and Corporate Relations

Appendix C Issues for Discussion

Session 1

1. What is the impact of the new technology on the cohesiveness of the campus community?

2. What is to be gained from integrating the computing resources—what do faculty really want?

3. What do faculty want to have provided to them as services and what do they want to do for themselves?

4. What effects will the linking of the university with the wider communities have such as with local technical organizations?

5. Is the technology causing or will it cause a gap between universities (faculty, administrators, and students) that have access to the technology as compared with those that do not have access?

6. What is the effect of workstation environments on student socialization? What is the impact on faculty-student relationships?

7. What is the socialization's impact on the technology—for example, what is the impact on standardization?

8. What is the role of the computing resource in the assistance to instruction?

9. What is the faculty member's role in providing an access service to a semiprivate database?

   a. What is the impact of this on faculty mobility?

   b. What is an adequate support mechanism?

10. What is the information content of the network and who is planning for it?

11. How is higher education going to cope collectively with these problems?

12. What expectations do we have and what educational requirements will be necessary for the knowledge worker of the future?

13. Will natural communities arise as a result of networking and can they be identified?

14. Organizational issues surrounding the ownership and responsibilities for maintaining the databases.

15. Power and authority implications of the new types of systems.

16. Legal and policy issues (copyright) are causing fundamental tensions between libraries, authors, and publishers. This had major impact on the value and thus the maintenance of the database.

    a. This raises issues of electronic publishing including pricing.

    b. What is the role of the higher education community in ensuring that these information and instructional elements are maintained in the marketplace?

    c. What are the evaluation issues of faculty, staff, and students in electronic publishing in computer-intensive environments?

17. How long is this transition and how do we cope in a multimobile environment—when is the future?

Session 2

1. How can the new librarian of the new library become a real colleague of the faculty member?

2. What is the cost of acquiring, storing and providing access to various kinds of information? What is the benefit? What must be given up to keep and use this information?

3. Is there something that libraries can or should do differently given the availability of the new more powerful and less expensive technology? What organizational changes (if any) are necessary?

4. Can we collaborate or must we cope collectively?

5. By following the old algorithms for controlling and providing access to information and given that we are already overwhelmed by that information, how can we provide users with the ability to filter the information adequately to optimize their time and capabilities?

Session 3

1. The universities that have been invited to this conference are regarded as the flagship institutions and the innovators and thus have been capable of acquiring major funding from foundation and university sponsors. How can universities that are not so regarded acquire the capital (and operating) funding for the creation of the future campus information environment (including the telecommunications network)?

2. How do we justify the future campus information environment?

   • Will the access to information be more efficient?
   • Will greater research productivity result?
   • Will greater educational (teaching?) productivity result?
   • How will we measure these?
   • What information resources from outside your campus will be required?
   • Will the information resources require additional funding?
   • How can we do this in a period of declining enrollment?

3. Can we afford to retain the current campus information procedures and services offered by our "traditional" campus information environments?

4. What are the areas of collaboration that are economically justifiable? That will help us more than just cope? That will assist in the identification of required standards?

5. Are we using the technology to improve what we are already doing or are we fundamentally changing the methods by which we achieve our goals?

Appendix D Selected References

Abell, M., and J. Coolman. "Professionals and Productivity: Keys to the Future of Academic Library and Information Services," In *Priorities for Academic Libraries*. New Directions for Higher Education, edited by Thomas Galvin and Beverly Lynch, no. 39, 71–86. San Francisco: Jossey-Bass, 1982.

Bailey, R. L. *Information Systems and Technological Decisions: A Guide for Nontechnical Administrators*. AAHE-ERIC/Higher Education Research Report No. 8, 1982. Washington, D.C.: American Association for Higher Education, 1982.

Balkovich, E., S. Lerman, and R. P. Parmelee. "Computing in Higher Education: The Athena Experience." *Communications of the ACM* 28 (November 1985): 1214–24.

Baron, N. S. "Priesthood and Pedagogy: Examining Presuppositions." *EDUCOM Bulletin* 20 (Winter 1985): 13–16.

Battin, P. "Crossing the Border: Librarianship in the Information Age." *The Harvard Librarian* 19 (September 1985): 8–10.

_____ . "The Electronic Library–A Vision for the Future." *EDUCOM Bulletin* 19 (Summer 1984): 12–17.

_____ . "Libraries, Computers, and Scholarship." *Wilson Library Bulletin* 56 (April 1982): 580–83.

_____ . "Libraries, Technology and Scholarship: The Library as an Information Center." IBM-ACIS Seminar, University Presidents and Chancellors, July 17, 1985.

_____ . "The Library: Center of the Restructured University." In *Current Issues in Higher Education,* edited by M. S. Tucker, no. 2, 25-31. Washington, D.C.: American Association for Higher Education, 1983–84.

Bok, D. "Looking into Education's High-Tech Future." *EDUCOM Bulletin* 20 (Fall 1985): 115–20.

Borgman, C. L., D. O. Case, and D. Ingebretsen. "University Faculty Use of Computerized Databases: An Assessment of Needs and Resources." *Online Review* 9(1985): 307–31.

Brown, J. S. "Process versus Product: A Perspective on Tools for Communal and Informal Electronic Learning." In *Education in the Electronic Age: A Report from the Learning Lab,* 41–58. New York: WNET/Thirteen Learning Lab, 1983.

Brown, M. H., N. Meyrowitz, and A. van Dam. "Personal Computer Networks and Graphical Animation: Rationale and Practice for Education." In *The Papers of the Fourteenth SIGCSE Technical Symposium on Computer Science Education,* edited by Sheau-Dong Lang. SIGCSE Bulletin, vol. 15, no. 1, 296–307. New York: Association for Computing Machinery, 1983.

Cleveland, H. "Educating for the Information Society." *Change* 17 (July/August 1985): 13–21.

Cotton, C. J., and N. M. Minnich. "A Local Area Network Based Computing Laboratory at the University of Delaware: Development and Impact on Campus Area Computing." In *Proceedings of the Twenty-Seventh IEEE Computer Society International Conference,* 100–107. Silver Spring, Md.: IEEE Computer Society Press, 1983.

Crecine, J. P. "The Role of Universities in Knowledge Dissemination: Site Licensing Is Secondary." *EDUCOM Bulletin* 20 (Summer 1985): 2–5.

Cyert, R. M. "New Teacher's Pet: The Computer." *IEEE Spectrum* 21 (June 1984): 120–22.

Danielson, W. "A Report from the Barricades of the Computer Revolution on Campus." *EDUCOM Bulletin* 20 (Winter 1985): 17–18.

DeGennaro, R. *Into the Information Age, Report of the Director of Libraries, University of Pennsylvania,* 1982-83. Philadelpha, Pa.: University of Pennsylvania, 1984.

———. "Libraries, Technology, and the Information Marketplace." *Library Journal* 107 (June 1, 1982): 1045–54.

Final Report of the Presidential Task Force on Information Processing. Patricia Battin, Chair. New York: Columbia University, April 1984.

Fleit, L. H. "Choosing a Chief Information Officer." *AAHE Bulletin* 38 (April 1986): 7–10.

Friedman, E. A. "The Wired University." *IEEE Spectrum* 21 (November 1984): 115–120.

Gilbert, S. W., and K. C. Green. "New Computing in Higher Education." *Change* 18 (May/June 1986): 33–50.

Glicksman, M. "Goals, Academic Direction, and Faculty Development." In *Leadership Roles of Chief Academic Officers.* New Directions for Higher Education, edited by David G. Brown, no. 47, 77–83. San Francisco: Jossey-Bass, 1984.

Goodman, H. J. A., and O. Standera. "An Exploration of Problems, Issues, and Prospects in the Sharing of Multi-Media Educational Resources Via Interactive Electronic Networks Which Involve the Use of Mini- and/or Micro-Computers." In *Proceedings of the Application of Mini- and Micro-Computer in Information, Documentation and Libraries International Conference,* edited by Carl Keren and Linda Perlmutter, 309–22. Amsterdam: North-Holland, 1983.

Henderson, R. P. "View From the Corporate Sector." *American Education* 18 (August/September 1982): 35–37.

Inman, B. R. "Emerging Technologies in Higher Education." *EDUCOM Bulletin* 20 (Winter 1985): 2–5.

Karr, R. D. "Using the Academic Computer Center." *College and Research Libraries News* 45 (September 1984): 411–14.

King, D. W., N. K. Roderer, and H. A. Olsen, eds. *Key Papers in the Economics of Information.* White Plains, N.J.: Knowledge Industry Publications for the American Society for Information Science, 1983.

Lancaster, F. W., and L. C. Smith. "Science, Scholarship and the Communication of Knowledge." *Library Trends* 27 (Winter 1979): 367–88.

Linvill, J. G. "University Role in the Computer Age." *Science* 215 (February 1982): 802–6.

Lipson, J. "Riding the Wave of the New Information Technologies: The Administrator's Role." *EDUCOM Bulletin* 16 (1981): 7–11.

Lynch, B. "Options for the 80's: Directions in Academic and Research Libraries." *College and Research Libraries* 43 (March 1982): 124–29.

McCredie, J. W., ed. *Campus Computing Strategies.* Bedford, Mass: Digital Equipment Corporation, 1983.

McCredie, J. W., and W. P. Timlake. "Evolving Computer Networks in American Higher Education." *EDUCOM Bulletin* 18 (Summer 1983): 5–10, 15.

Mein, B. "The Computerization of a Campus: A Trilogy." In *The Papers of the Sixteenth SIGCSE Technical Symposium on Computer Science Education,* edited by Harriet G. Taylor. SIGCSE Bulletin, vol. 17, no. 1, 221–6. New York: Association for Computing Machinery, 1985.

Meyrowitz, N. *Networks of Scholars' Workstations: End-User Computing in a University Community.* IRIS Technical Report, 85–3. Providence, R.I.: Brown University, Institute Research in Information and Scholarship, 1985.

Moran, B. B. *Academic Libraries: The Changing Knowledge Centers of College and Universities.* ASHE-ERIC Higher Education Research Report No. 8, 1984. Washington, D.C.: Association for the Study of Higher Education, 1984.

Morris, J. H., et al. "Andrew: A Distributed Personal Computing Environment." *Communications of the ACM* 29 (March 1986): 184–201.

Muller, S. "The Post-Gutenberg University." In *Current Issues in Higher Education,* edited by Russell Edgerton, no. 1, 32-38. Washington, D.C.: American Association for Higher Education, 1983–84.

Neff, R. K. "Merging Libraries and Computer Centers: Manifest Destiny or Manifestly Deranged?" *EDUCOM Bulletin* 20 (Winter 1985): 8–12, 16.

Oettinger, A. G. "Information Resources: Knowledge and Power in the 21st Century." *Science* 209 (July 1980): 191–8.

O'Neil, R. M. "Academic Libraries and the Future: A President's View." *College and Research Libraries* 45 (May 1984): 184–88.

Plane, R. A. "Books, Libraries, Scholarship and the Future." In *Priorities for Academic Libraries.* New Directions for Higher Education, edited by Thomas Galvin and Beverly Lynch, no. 39, 89–96. San Francisco: Jossey-Bass, 1982.

Ploch, M. "Micros Flood Campuses." *High Technology* 4 (March 1984): 47–49.

Preliminary Report: The Future of Computing at Carnegie-Mellon University, Allen Newell, Chairman. Pittsburgh, Pa: The Task Force for the Future of Computing, Carnegie-Mellon University, February 1982.

"Project Athena: An Introduction." Cambridge, Mass.: The Massachusetts Institute of Technology, October 1983.

Rauch-Hindin, W. "Universities Are Setting Trends in Data Communications Nets." *Data Communications* 10 (October 1981): 64–79.

Schure, A. "From the Chair of the Presidency." *College and Research Libraries* 36 (May 1975): 188–92.

Sethna, B., V. Dubrovsky, and S. Kolla. "Implications of the Impact of 'Extensive' Computerization on an Organization." In *Proceedings of the International Congress on Technology & Technology Exchange,* 396–97. New York: IEEE, 1984.

Shank, R. "New Expectations from Users of Academic Libraries." In *Priorities for Academic Libraries.* New Directions for Higher Education, edited by Thomas Galvin and Beverly Lynch, no. 39. San Francisco: Jossey-Bass, 1982.

Shipp, W.S., N. Meyrowitz, and A. van Dam. "Networks of Scholars' Workstations in a University Community." In *Proceedings of the Twenty-Seventh IEEE Computer Society International Conference,* 108–22. Silver Spring, Md.: IEEE Computer Society Press, 1983.

Shipp, W. S., and H. H. Webber. "The Brown University Network–Brunet." In *Proceedings of the Twenty-Fifth IEEE Computer Society International Conference,* 255–61. New York: IEEE, 1982.

———. "Wiring a University." In *IEEE 1982 International Conference on Communications, The Digital Revolution.* New York: IEEE, 1982.

Slack, K., J. Morris, D. Van Houweling, and N. Wishbow. "The Future of Computing at Carnegie-Mellon University." In *Proceedings of the Twenty-Seventh IEEE Computer Society International Conference,* 94–99. Silver Spring, Md.: IEEE Computer Society Press, 1983.

Spinrad, R. J. "The Electronic University." *EDUCOM Bulletin* 18 (Fall/Winter 1983): 4–8.

Stevenson, M. B. "Information and the Academic Community." *Aslib Proceedings* 32 (1980): 78–81.

Talbot, R. J. "Financing the Academic Library." In *Priorities for Academic Libraries.* New Directions for Higher Education, edited by Thomas Galvin and Beverly Lynch, no. 39, 35–44. San Francisco: Jossey-Bass, 1982.

Tate, P. J., and M. Kressel, eds. *The Expanding Role of Telecommunications in Higher Education*. New Directions for Higher Education, no. 44. San Francisco: Jossey-Bass, 1983.

Tucker, M. S. "The Turning Point: Telecommunications and Higher Education." In *The Expanding Role of Telecommunications in Higher Education*. New Directions for Higher Education, edited by Pamela J. Tate and Marilyn Kressel, no. 44, 11–21. San Francisco: Jossey-Bass, 1983.

Tucker, M. S. "Computers on Campus: Working Papers." In *Current Issues in Higher Education,* edited by M. S. Tucker, no. 2. Washington, D.C.: American Association for Higher Education, 1983–84.

Turock, B. J. "Technology and the Post-Industrial Society: The Academic Library in the 1980s and Beyond." *Catholic Library World* 55 (February 1984): 298–304.

Updegrove, D. A. "Computer-Intensive Campuses: Strategies, Plans, Implications." *EDUCOM Bulletin* 21 (Spring 1986): 11–14.

VanHorn, R. L. "Vignette: Carnegie-Mellon and IBM Cooperate for Networked Personal Computing." *Educational Record* 64 (Fall 1983): 6–8.

Wilkinson, J. "Beyond the Computer—." *Canadian Library Journal* 41 (October 1984): 243–47.

"The 'Wired University' Is on the Way." *Business Week* (April 1982): 68–69.

Wollitzer, P. "Faculty Perspectives on Computer-Based Education: Current Status and Future Prospects in Higher Education." *Journal of Computer Based Instruction* 3 (February 1977): 76–83.

Yankelovich, N., N. Meyrowitz, and A. van Dam. "Reading and Writing the Electronic Book." *Computer* 18 (October 1985): 15–29.

Young, J. S. "Hypermedia." *MacWorld* 3 (March 1986): 116–21.